EVEN IF YOU WERE PERFECT,
Someone Would Crucify You

This book reads like you were hanging out talking to Rob one on one. Just like Rob, it is honest, funny, and challenging. I've seen the effects of people pleasing in my own life and the lives of others and its extremely dangerous. Rob gives us a valuable tool to help us navigate these "chummy" waters. Good stuff Rob!

—Chad Childress
Struggling People Pleaser and Director of Missionary and Church Development for the North American Mission Board

Rob Shepherd's book *Even if You Were Perfect Someone Would Crucify You* confirmed what I already knew…I'm not perfect. In short, digestible chapters Shepherd shares several truths every human needs to know: don't take yourself too seriously, there will always be critics, and your identity must be found in Jesus! You'll enjoy reading & laughing your way through this book!

—Terrace Crawford
Nationally Recognized Speaker & Author of *Going Social*

Rob Shepherd is one of the best writers and communicators in the church today. His voice needs to be heard and listened to. This book will nail you in regards to cutting out the paralyzing noises of life and opinions of others. Be ready for a tugging at your heart to rest and re-discover your identity FULLY in Him.

—Chad Johnson
Director of the Catalyst Conference

In *Even If You Were Perfect Someone Would Crucify You,* my friend Rob Shepherd goes beyond telling us not to try to please people. He inspires us to fall more in love with Jesus which in turn will help us care less about what people think and more about what Jesus does.

—Clayton King
Founder & President of Crossroads Ministries
Teaching Pastor @ Newspring Church, Campus Pastor @
Liberty University, Author for *Harvest House*

Should you read this book?

- If the title caught your attention, you should read this book. Every page is riveted to this central theme and the author shares a plethora of examples, and applications to free the chronic people pleaser.

- If you can tolerate serious thoughts presented with a wicked sense of humor, you should read this book.

- If you will not judge an author who dares to be transparent and share his own struggles, you should read this book.

- If you are not a grammar czar who objects to contractions, sudden changes in person from less personal "They" to the direct encounter "You", and do not condemn passive voice, you will enjoy the book.

- If you do not mind an author who uses big words like HUGE or Gigantor, you can manage this book.

- If you enjoy new vocabulary, like "schemy," not found in the dictionary, you should read this book.

- If you are a people pleaser or know someone who is, you should read this book.

EVEN IF YOU WERE PERFECT

Someone Would Crucify You

Stop trying to please people.
Start pleasing God

ROB SHEPHERD

NEW YORK

EVEN IF YOU WERE PERFECT,
Someone Would Crucify You
Stop trying to please people. Start pleasing God

ISBN 978-1-61448-513-1 paperback
ISBN 978-1-61448-514-8 eBook
Library of Congress Control Number: 2013930345

Morgan James Publishing
The Entrepreneurial Publisher
5 Penn Plaza, 23rd Floor
New York City, New York 10001
(212) 655-5470 office • (516) 908-4496 fax
www.MorganJamesPublishing.com

Cover Design by:
Rachel Lopez
www.r2cdesign.com

Interior Design by:
Bonnie Bushman
bonnie@caboodlegraphics.com

In an effort to support local communities, raise awareness and funds, Morgan James Publishing donates a percentage of all book sales for the life of each book to Habitat for Humanity Peninsula and Greater Williamsburg.

Get involved today, visit
www.MorganJamesBuilds.com.

To the members of Next Level Church, who have patiently walked with a pastor who still struggles with pleasing people, but desperately is seeking his identity in Jesus. I love being your pastor. Together we can change the world by loving Jesus, loving people, and making a difference.

Contents

Acknowledgments

To Monica, you have influenced my understanding of how much Jesus loves imperfect people by your constant love for me. It must be hard being married to a people pleasing, sensitive, incredibly good looking (for an overweight bald guy) pastor, but you make it seem easy. Thank you for loving me well, and for supporting my dream to write a book! I love God more because of you!

To my parents, who faithfully modeled a great marriage and a love for Jesus. I also would like to thank you for allowing us to move back in with you as we follow God's call to plant a church. You are a huge part of our story. Oh, and Mom, I know that you put in a lot of time editing this book. I greatly appreciate it! Thanks for making my writing look like I paid attention in English class.

To Reese and Hayden, I love being your dad. I know you can't read this now, but one day I hope that you will read the words that I try to live out every day. You both are more than sermon illustrations and blog material. You are proof that God answers prayer. I love you both!

To Jon, Nicole, Congo, and Brody, you are one of the main reasons why we planted a church in the 757. Monica and I love living life with you. We were willing to go anywhere God led us, but we are eternally grateful that we got the green light to stay close to you guys.

To Sarah, Scott, Selleck, Slade, and Sawyer, thanks for being our Ohio family. I hope that this book makes you proud of your little brother, brother-in-law, and uncle.

To Mark and Dodi, I know that it is scary to have a son-in-law who quits his job to plant a church with no guarantee of insurance or a salary. Thanks for not showing me your fear. I also want to thank you for producing my wife. She's awesome! Good job.

To Chad Johnson, thanks for being my best friend since eighth grade. Being a military kid, I never had a friend longer than a year. Meeting you at the cafeteria was a God thing.

To Dan and Danielle, your friendship and support mean more to me than you realize. Friends are more valuable to me than money. You bring a lot of worth to my life. I would also like to take this time to thank you in advance for taking the four of us in if the zombie apocalypse ever does happen.

To Courtney Hornsby, you were the first person to tell me to plant a church. You didn't know what God was stirring in my heart at the time. The fact that you were willing to move with us to plant a church helped me know that I wasn't crazy for wanting to do the impossible for God. Thanks for being a best friend to Monica, a Co-co to the twins, and a risk taker with me.

To Catalyst conference, you have done more for my leadership and passion for God than anything else period. God uses you each year to rock my world.

To Ben Arment, you will never get me to stop saying thank you for what you did for me. My life was radically changed because you believed in me. Thank you!

To Clayton King, thanks for taking time to invest in me. Thanks for being consistently passionate for Jesus! Thanks for praying that we would have twins. That still blows my mind!

To the staff at Next Level, you are sent from God. Never forget that we are not just doing church. We are the church. Thank you for putting up with a dreamer who lacks administrative skills. Thank you for being more about God's kingdom than your own. Thank you for taking initiative. Thank you for listening to God and starting a church! I'm honored to serve as your pastor. Oh, and this book won't be required reading for our staff meetings. And, yes, you will get a free copy.

To all my friends, I know that some of you will complain because your name wasn't mentioned specifically in this section. My response is, "Even if I wrote the perfect acknowledgements, someone would crucify me." I hope that you know that friendship matters to me. Whether we are friends from high school, college, seminary, or church, you have impacted my life. You have been the ones that I've worked so hard to please. You are the ones who have inspired so many life lessons. You have influenced my life and are therefore a huge part of this book.

To the readers of robshep.com, thank you for reading every day. Thank you for putting up with my poor grammar. Writing for you every day gave me the stamina to write a book. I am forever grateful for your comments and interactions. Thank you for being my online community!

Finally, I want to thank the wicked awesome team at Morgan James publishing. Thank you for taking a chance on a first time author. Thank you for the hours you spent making this book look way better than anything I could ever do on my own.

Introduction

If you want to make friends, there are a few polarizing topics that you should not bring up in your first introduction.

1. Politics – unless you are at a Republican or Democratic convention, it is wise to not bring up a preference for Fox News or MSNBC, donkeys or elephants, or your opinions on whether or not universal healthcare is a communist/Muslim/ antichrist plot to destroy the world. Just resist the urge to bring this up within the first 5 minutes of talking with someone.

2. Religion – religion is very polarizing. Now I'm not talking about being silent about Jesus. If God leads you to talk to someone about Jesus then you should do that. I'm talking about religious debates. If you want to make friends, don't lead with "Hi my name is _____ and I'm a Baptist/Charismatic/ 5 Point Calvinist/the antichrist!"

3. Nickleback – the band. Unless you enjoy getting beat up gang style, you should avoid saying "Nickelback is the greatest

band ever!" There are lots of people who feel like Nickelback is a sign of the end times and thus provides the soundtrack to the antichrist.

Not too long ago, I was talking with a friend about Nickelback, and I encouraged him not to post his feelings about the band on Facebook. He asked, "Why?" I told him that there are large groups of people who would rather cut off their ears than burn in the fires of Nickelback.

According to Urban Dictionary, the definition of Nickelback is "the act of willfully allowing one's ears to bleed." An example of this is "I was Nickelbacking, so the school nurse sent me home early."

I ended up asking my Facebook friends how they feel about Nickelback. I was surprised at what I found. Out of the 28 comments, only 6 hated on Nickelback. Most of those who hated on them were musicians themselves. Those who hated on them really loathed them. At the same time, the vast majority of people said that they love them.

Nickelback has sold 50 million albums, yet if you follow pop culture, they've brought about as much to the music scene as William Hung from American Idol. Google him to get the full effect of that statement.

It's interesting to me how loud a negative voice is. Haters are going to hate and when they do, it's as if they carry a megaphone.

Think about the power of words. One negative word outweighs hundreds of positive words. In other words, one positive word doesn't erase the effects of one negative word. In fact, some really smart people who have doctorates have said that it takes 5 positive words to offset one negative word. Studies have shown that the brain actually has a "negativity bias." Our brains actually focus on the negative over the positive.

We as humans are fragile, and it doesn't take much to break us. Words are power. The truth is there are more people that love Nickelback then those that hate them. The hate is so strong because negative words weigh more. Please know that this is not an endorsement for all things Nickelback. I personally think a lot of their lyrics are polished off smut that gets past the radio censors. My point is not that they are a good band or not. My point is that in our culture it feels like they are the worst thing since shoulder pads were in all ladies' clothes.

Whether it's Nickleback, the New York Yankees, the movie *Titanic*, or you, all have something in common. They are very popular, yet someone still found a way to hate on them. I know you might not want to think that you have anything in common with Nickleback, but you do. The truth is no matter how many people like you, someone will find a way to hate on you. You can either let it destroy you or try something greater. That's the goal of this book. It is not to ignore the ones who will criticize us. It is to find our identity in someone so great that we can overcome even the greatest hater. It is my prayer that every person who reads this falls more in love with Jesus. It's through Jesus that we can learn to be okay with the fact that even if we were perfect, someone would crucify us.

Chapter One

Even if You Were Perfect, Someone Would Crucify You

You've faced it. If you have one of those Twitters or Facebooks, you've faced it. If you are reading this in the future, and Twitter and Facebook don't exist, you've still faced it. Whenever you future people picked out your first hover board or flying car, you faced it. If you own 1.21 gigawatts and use it to go back in time and have a copy of this book, you faced it on your MySpace page. If you are a pastor or a teacher, you've faced it. If you've ever cooked a meal for anyone other than yourself, you've faced it. If you've tried a new haircut, gone to public school, had a kid, visited a place where there is a different accent, worn a fanny pack, or shown someone your high school yearbook, then you've faced it. At some point in life, everyone has faced negative comments from people. When negativity hits you, it hurts like a mother.

The inspiration for this book came from a very hurtful place. I had preached a sermon on relationships, and someone didn't like it. In fact, this someone didn't like it so much he/she decided to write me an anonymous letter. I should have known that it was trouble, but I was actually excited to receive a real life letter. People don't write those any more. I mean it takes time to use ancient things such as pen and paper. Oh, and to send it, you need a stamp, so it costs something.

It didn't dawn on me that such glorious attention could be filled with negativity until I was well into the first paragraph. The letter was dripping with crazy. It said things about being thankful our local news media wasn't there to get coverage of the talk. The local media was never at our church. I don't know where the writer came up with that one. The person wrote that he could tell that everyone around him hated the talk as much as he did. It was four pages of abuse, but I couldn't stop reading it.

It didn't matter that I had received close to twenty emails from people telling me that God spoke to them. It didn't matter that my wife, parents, and church staff liked the talk. It didn't matter that I did my best, or that I said what I thought God was leading me to say. All that mattered was that some anonymous stranger didn't like my message. His insults consumed me.

On the fourth reading, I sensed a still small voice say to me, "Even if you preached a perfect sermon, someone would crucify it." I immediately balled up the letter and threw it away. I was allowing someone I didn't know to define me. I was allowing someone who didn't have the guts to confront me, to change the entire outcome of what had been a great day.

The truth is, it wasn't a perfect sermon. I'm not perfect. The truth is, even if it was the perfect sermon, someone would have found something wrong with it. The truth is, I was living to please people.

What I learned is an ancient truth expressed well by John Lundgate, a fourteenth century monk. "You can please some of the people some of the time, some of the people all of the time, but you can never please all of the people all of the time." I can't please all people all the time, so I should instead live to please God.

This is my story. I'm a recovering people pleaser. One of my greatest addictions in life is having people say nice things about me. I love it. However, when something doesn't go my way, it brutally destroys my self worth. I'm thankful that God spoke louder than the voice in that anonymous letter.

A New Perspective

Since I heard that voice about crucifying sermons, I've adapted that phrase to multiple areas of my life. *Even if you were perfect, someone would crucify you.* This phrase helps me not to be defined by the opinions of others.

The only perfect person who ever lived is Jesus. He was without sin. Yet, humans found a way to have him brutally punished by one of the severest death penalties a government has ever issued. Man-kind crucified a perfect Savior, and we've been verbally crucifying people ever since. Whether it's crucifying ourselves because we don't live up to the way other people might see us, or it's having our hard work crucified because someone doesn't like it, we face verbal crucifixions on a regular basis. At the end of the day, we must conclude that we can't please all people all of the time.

We can only live our lives in a way that pleases God. Rick Warren once tweeted, "Even God can't please everyone. Only fools try to do what God can't." Ouch.

This book is for my fellow people pleasers. Maybe that's not you. If not, then please pass this book to someone who struggles with the pressure to please others. I wish that I didn't care so much about people's opinions. I wish I could be that guy who goes to the grocery store wearing a high school t-shirt, sweatpants, and a fanny pack. You know who I'm talking about? There seems to be one in every city. That joker doesn't care what others think. I am not that joker. I care. I also don't own a fanny pack.

This book isn't a self help book. It's about finding identity in Jesus. When we see ourselves as God sees us, we realize the truth: On our good days, we aren't as great as we think we are, and on our bad days, we aren't as pathetic. We are each in need of a Savior, redemption, and grace. This is my story, and I hope that through it you will be empowered to deflect verbal crucifixions. I hope that through this book you will find freedom in knowing: *Even if you were perfect, someone would crucify you.*

Chapter Two

Identity Theft

I have a friend that I will call Ryan. I will call him Ryan because that's his name. Well, Ryan calls me one day in a panic. Someone had stolen Ryan's identity. We were supposed to hang out that night, but he didn't expect such a crisis. It was a mess. He was stressed like a new dad in a delivery room. His life was forever changed because someone had stolen his identity. I asked Ryan what this thief bought with the stolen identity. I expected to hear a long list of items like a new car, a cruise, gold plated Spanx, a unicorn, and a lifetime supply of Chick-fil-A. Mmmm...Chick-fil-A! My expectations were destroyed when Ryan tells me that this thief purchased a credit score report and twelve of his fifteen dollars from an iTunes gift card. DO WHAT?! I couldn't help but laugh. Ryan was worked up over a credit score and a few bucks on iTunes. I'm not even sure that was identity theft. I think it was identity confusion. Someone had to have made a mistake. I mean, if you are going to steal someone's identity, you better at least do a shopping spree at Wal-Mart. Why risk jail time for a credit report?

My laughter didn't help Ryan. He felt violated. Still to this day, he brings up this incident as if he was seriously victimized. I guess, in a sense, he was. Someone bought something under Ryan's name, but I still think it's funny.

The Bible says, "You were bought at a price; do not become slaves of human beings" (1 Corinthians 7:23). Now, it's clear from the context that the author was talking about physical slavery. In America, slavery is no longer acceptable, but that doesn't mean that people are truly free. I think that this verse can apply to stolen identity.

I counseled someone once who was going through a really difficult time. She had recently been divorced, but that wasn't what was rocking her world. Her former spouse was saying incredibly hurtful things to her. He was saying that he had already found someone who met his needs more than she did. He knew exactly what to say to destroy her, and it was hitting her like a cannon ball. The kicker was that she was lonely and was actually considering going back to him. I asked her what her identity was found in. She looked at me as if I asked her if she prefers Vulcans or Romulans from *Star Trek*. She was dazed and confused by my question. I asked her again, and she stumbled through her answer. After she answered, I told her why I asked. Here was a guy who abused her their entire marriage. To make matters worse, he would verbally abuse her and use the Bible to justify his actions. She finally got the guts to leave him, and now she was actually thinking about going back to him. On a side note, I do think that God's ultimate plan would be for this couple to get back together, but not until he repents and truly changes. Staying in an abusive relationship is not healthy. God hates divorce, but that doesn't mean that you can't get out of harm's way while praying that God truly changes your spouse. I digress. This woman couldn't sleep at night because her former husband said incredibly hurtful things to her. She was already in counseling, but nothing was helping her. I told her that I thought her identity was her ex-husband. When our identity is wrapped up in someone else, we can't function normally. This woman was actually thinking about going back to the abuse, just so her ex wouldn't be with another woman. She was a slave to his opinions of her. His opinion of her mattered more than her physical well being. It even mattered more than her kids. She was going to bring her kids back to him, even though he didn't have custody and was pure evil to them. The problem is her identity wasn't his to abuse. She was bought at a price, by Jesus.

The truth is, no matter how good you are, someone will make fun of you. No matter how hard you try, someone won't like you. *Even if you were perfect...*

Question time! Whose opinion matters more to you than it should? For example, if this person doesn't give you the reaction that you want, it wrecks you. Who has power to ruin your day with words? What do you do to seek validation? Why can't you forgive someone who hurt you?

Maybe I'm alone in this people pleasing thing, but if you know the answers to some of these questions then you may be a victim of identity theft. The Bible says, "Am I now trying to win the approval of people or of God? Or am I trying to please people? If I were still trying to please people, I would not be Christ's servant" (Galatians 1:10).

Let that verse sink in. We can't be Christ's servants when we are slaves to other people's opinions.

A Servant of Christ

Here are some signs of a stolen identity:

- You don't spend time reading the Bible because you don't have time. It's crazy that you make time for other things, but won't make time for Jesus. This is an issue of stolen identity. We prioritize what's important to us.

- Your personality changes, depending on who you are hanging out with.
- Your insecurities are magnified around certain people.
- Nobody knows the real you.
- You make decisions based solely on the opinions of others. For example, you can't leave the house without make-up because people would see the real you.
- You don't spend significant time praying or even thinking about God. Instead, you spend significant time thinking about the opinions of others.
- You can't confess your sins to others because you are afraid you will be judged.
- You allow jealousy to ruin relationships. You can't truly be happy for others because you wish their good was happening to you.
- You can't say, "No."
- You feel the pressure to lie about things like your age, weight, or the college you went to because you want to impress people.
- You buy things that you cannot afford because it makes you feel worthy.

If one or more of those is true of you then you are a victim of stolen identity. Because we can't please everyone, we have two options. We can continue fighting furiously to win people over, or we can find our identity in Jesus. He bought us at a price. He died for us. We belong to God! So it's time to stop allowing others to steal our identity. It's time to find our identity in Jesus. The question is, how do we do that?

Chapter Three

It Starts with God

In middle school, I discovered insecurity. Or, maybe, it discovered me. I am not only a people pleaser, I am also all about words of affirmation. In middle school, there aren't a lot of words of affirmation being thrown at you. There are, however, group showers after PE class. The only reason I survived is because I refused to take a shower. That's right. I stank! I changed clothes by myself in the handicap stall. Thank God for handicap stalls. They are much larger and come with hooks on the doors for clothes. I'm kind of a germaphobe, so the hooks were crucial. I believe that there's a reason why private parts are called private, and I plan on keeping it that way. I sprayed on extra deodorant and then added some Old Spice cologne to cover my stank. Yes I wrote stank. It's worse than stink. I'm sure nobody could tell. I would convince myself of this when our class received the hygiene speech from one of our teachers. Lucky for me no one ever called me out. I wasn't called out because no one noticed. I would get in and get out of that stall like a ninja on fire. It was fast and furious.

My insecurity continued strong through high school. The problem was that I overvalued some people's opinions. I would be shy around people that I thought were cool but more confident around those that…well…weren't a threat to my security. At school, I was a shy, reserved teenager. At the exact same time, I was in a band, led a sixth grade Sunday school class, and was full of life at my church youth group.

Many people think that shyness is a result of being introverted. It can be, but it's not always the case. An introvert receives energy from alone time. An extrovert receives energy from being around people. Shyness is different because it's lacking confidence to be yourself around others. Shyness is a type of fear that paralyzes us from being our true selves. We become afraid of what others will say about us, so our best defense is to say nothing.

How do I know this? I know this because there are some people who slap me silly with shyness. This is why for years I thrived working with teenagers. For some reason, I had confidence working with teens at my church. They liked me. I could be silly and be myself. However, when I was around a peer I thought was cool, I became camouflaged. In other words, I would pick a wall and lean on it—hoping that I wouldn't have to speak. If I didn't talk, then I couldn't say something stupid. My insecurity generated my shyness.

My favorite band of all time is dc Talk. You may not have heard of them, but they were HUGE when I was in high school. The day before my senior year of high school, a friend and I drove three hours to see them in concert. We got to the show early and just happened to see their sound check. It was an outdoor concert, so even though they didn't let us in the venue, we could watch them from the other side of a fence. They finished their sound check, and something happened to make me giddier than a woman at Target. The band members of dc Talk started walking towards me. It was glorious. My buddy and I had rehearsed what we would say to them if we got a chance to talk to them. When my favorite member of the band, Tobymac, came walking towards me, I froze in fear. I became incredibly shy. I couldn't think of my questions. Toby walks past me, and I see that I'm about to lose my chance to talk with him. I finally get the confidence to blurt something out. It was one of those times when I wish I could have pulled the words back as they left my mouth. I yelled at Tobymac, "REMEMBER ME!" I honestly don't know if it was a statement or a question. I had met him one time before when I was in fifth grade but, let's be honest, he wasn't going to remember that. I also like the idea of him remembering me in the future but, let's be honest, I don't want him remembering this encounter. It was so embarrassing. He smiled, politely, and then hustled on like he was escaping a stalker. Why couldn't I have just been myself? It is moments like that, and many others, that made my true self hide inside and not want to come out and play. Still to this day, if I meet someone I highly appreciate, I have to pray and ask God to help me be myself. I could be shy and not say something stupid, but then I miss meeting someone new. I would rather be myself. I would rather be myself and not blurt out stupid things.

A Power Struggle

"It is not on what we spend the greatest amount of time that molds us the most, but whatever exerts the most power over us" O.Chambers.

What exerts the most power over you? Answering that question is important if you want to find your identity. Think about what consumes your thoughts. Is it money? Is it pleasure? Is it something that you don't have? Is it sports? Is it the weekend? Is it other people? Is it Jesus?

My identity has a foundation. It starts with Jesus. From there, I have other things that are a part of my identity, but it's impossible to separate who I am from Jesus. I am a HUGE Lakers fan. I love movies! I'm a proud dad to Reese and Hayden. I passionately love my wife. I eat Chipotle once a week because it's amazing. In fact, I believe that Chipotle has healing powers. I once came home from a trip to Mexico and had the worst rumbly in my tumbly. It was brutal. Nothing could fix it. Nothing, except Chipotle. I ate a Chipotle burrito and then returned to my regularly scheduled bowel movements. I digress.

The point is, there are lots of things that contribute to who I am. When people describe me, they will mention some of the things I listed. When people talk about you, they will, no doubt, talk about some of your passions, interests, and loves. However, everything starts with finding your identity in Jesus! It's all about Him. I can't separate whose I am, from who I am.

The sad thing is that way too many of us are finding our identities in weak foundations. We find our identity in our stuff, our reputation, or other people. We may become crushed, depressed, or consumed with negativity when our foundation falters. In other words when money isn't flowing, when stuff breaks, or when someone lets us down, it wrecks us.

A Solid Foundation

Look at what Jesus says about foundations in the Bible:

Therefore everyone who hears these words of mine and puts them into practice is like a wise man who built his house on the rock. The rain came down, the streams rose, and the winds blew and beat against that house; yet it did not fall, because it had its foundation on the rock. But everyone who hears these words of mine and does not put them into practice is like a foolish man who built his house on sand" (Matthew 7:24-26).

When you apply Jesus' teachings, you set up a solid foundation. Applying Jesus' teaching is doing more than just hearing it. It's doing what He says. In order to do what He says, you have to believe that He is right. In other words when your identity is in Jesus, a sign of it is obedience. This is HUGE. A benefit to obeying Jesus is a solid foundation—a foundation that does not shift or collapse. It's a foundation that can withstand personal attacks, broken dreams, and other storms that life throws your way. Don't skim over this too quickly. When your identity is in anything but Jesus, it can't reliably support you.

When I received that anonymous letter, it could have consumed me for days, instead of minutes. Someone attacked me. Someone attacked me, personally. For me, understanding that, *Even if I was perfect, someone would crucify me,* gave me freedom. It gave me freedom because I can't please all people at all times. Did it sting? Heck to the yes. It hurt for a few seconds, but I was able to sleep that night because ultimately I know that Jesus is my foundation. I can't please all people, all of the time. That means that a storm will sometimes strike in the form of negative people who will attack me. I can let it consume me, or I can understand it for what it is. It's wind. It's thunder. It's a storm, but it's not going to beat me down.

So look at your life. What causes your life to crumble? I'm talking about what keeps you up at night with worry? What has happened to you that makes it difficult for you to stand? That's your foundation, and it's faulty. It stinks. It's not worth building on. On the other hand, when Jesus is your foundation, you can withstand personal attacks.

So how do you make Jesus your foundation? According to Jesus, you listen to what He says, and then put His words into practice. I wonder if personal attacks hurt so much because we don't really know what Jesus says? When was the last time you soaked in Jesus' words like a good book, or in my case a great movie? I'd rather watch the movie than read the book, any day. The movie version of this book is going to rock your world, little country girl. It's going to star Will Smith, as me. Why are you laughing? Okay, there won't be a movie of this book, but if there was, it would star Will Smith, have ninjas, and be in 6D. That's three times greater than 3D.

Challenge Time

Here's a challenge for you: Spend time reading Jesus' words, thinking about Jesus' words, and then living out Jesus' words. Make some time every day to soak in what Jesus says. If you don't know where to start, then start with the first book in the New Testament—*Matthew*. From there read *Mark*, *Luke*, and *John*. Read a chapter a day. Read two chapters a day. Read five verses a day. The point isn't how much you read. The point is to read what Jesus says and build your foundation by doing it. Before you read, ask God to speak to your heart. Ask Him to soften your heart so that you can hear what He wants to say to you. After you read, ask yourself what the verses say about God? Ask yourself what the verses challenge you to do. Get to know God, and build your foundation.

Chapter Four

God is Not All
that You Need

This chapter is scary for me to write. People may take this chapter out of context. I may be crucified over this chapter. I hope that people will read the whole chapter and not just the title. At the end of the day though, even if I wrote the perfect book, someone would crucify it.

Your foundation starts with God. When it comes to salvation, it's all about God. True happiness, purpose, and meaning come from giving God glory. But it's my understanding from the Bible that God didn't wire you to be alone. I think that God, Himself, showed us that He's not all that we need.

The book of Genesis is the first book of the Bible. It's where we get the creation account of how God created the world. It goes something like this…God created something and then said it was good. God took pride in His creation—not pride in a negative way, but pride in a holy way—like the pride parents feel in their children. Therefore, God creates the stars, waters, trees, animals and declares that they are all good. He then creates man and look at what the Bible says, "The Lord God said, 'It is not good for the man to be alone. I will make a helper suitable for him' " (Genesis 2:18).

Did you catch what God said? It's the first time that God looks at His creation and says, "It's not good. It's not good for man to be alone." But the man wasn't alone. He had animals, including "man's best friend." He also had Satan's best friend the cat. I kid, I kid. He could have been a tree hugger and had an oak as a best friend. What's really interesting to me is that God was with Adam. God walked in the garden with Adam. Adam wasn't alone. He had God. In fact, Adam had a one on one relationship with God, and God says, "It's not good. It's not good for man to be alone." That was true in the garden, and it's true today.

People Are Really Important

You see, the solution to finding our identity isn't throwing out all people and only having a relationship with God. It's finding God as our foundation, so that we can have healthy relationships with others.

When I read through the Bible, I continually see how important people are to God and also to us. Jesus was once asked, "What is the greatest commandment?" Look at how He responds. Jesus says, "Love the Lord your God with all your heart and with all your soul and with all your mind. This is the first and greatest commandment. And the second is like it: 'Love your neighbor as yourself.' All the Law and the Prophets hang on these two commandments" (Matthew 22:37-40).

So the first commandment is to love God with all of our heart, soul, and mind. That makes sense to me. But what was the second? "Love your neighbor as yourself." Jesus says the second command is like the first. How is loving my neighbor like loving God? It seems to me that there is a connection between our love for God and our love for people. In fact, you can't say that you love God if you are not loving other people. 1 John 1:5-7 says, "This is the message we have heard from him and declare to you: God is light; in him there is no darkness at all. If we claim to have fellowship with him yet walk in the darkness, we lie and do not live by the truth. But if we walk in the light, as he is in the light, we have fellowship with one another, and the blood of Jesus, his Son, purifies us from all sin."

Okay, so God is light. And a sign of us walking in the light is that we will have fellowship with one another. There is a connection between our love for God and our love for people. Still not convinced? 1 John 2:9-11 says, "Anyone who claims to be in the light but hates his brother is still in the darkness. Whoever loves his brother lives in the light, and there is nothing in him to make him stumble. But whoever hates his brother is in the darkness and walks around in the darkness; he does not know where he is going, because the darkness has blinded him."

We can't be in the light and hate another human. There is a connection between our relationship with God and our relationship with people. 1 John 3:10 says, "This is how we know who the children of God are and who the children of the devil are: Anyone who does not do what is right is not a child of God; nor is anyone who does not love his brother."

Jesus took this really seriously. Matthew 5:22-24 says, "But I tell you that anyone who is angry with his brother will be subject to judgment. Again, anyone who says to his brother, 'Raca,' is answerable to the Sanhedrin. But anyone who says, 'You fool!' will be in danger of the fire of hell. "Therefore, if you are offering your gift at the altar and there remember that your brother has something against you, leave your gift there in front of the altar. First go and be reconciled to your brother; then come and offer your gift."

Did you catch that? Jesus says that anyone who is angry with his brother will be subject to judgment. He then says that if you are offering a gift at the altar and remember that someone has a beef with you, you are to leave your gift at the altar and go reconcile your relationship. So let me get this straight. We are to put our worship of God on hold until we have a right relationship with others? That's intense.

Think about it. How important are humans to God's plan? God could use any method that He wants for people to hear about Him. He could use fire from heaven, talking animals, or words written in the clouds. God could tell us about Himself any way that He wants, yet He chooses to use humans. This is HUGE! I can't tell you how many times people tell me that they used to believe in God, but they don't anymore because of the actions of others. I've had conversations with people who struggled to relate to God, the Father, because their earthly father was awful. On the flip side, I've had people fall in love with Jesus because of the irresistible love shown to them by a Christian. We are the hands and feet of God. Our action toward others matters because it reflects our God.

You see, *Even if You Were Perfect, Someone Would Crucify You* is not meant to be a write off of humans. We need other humans. In fact, God wired us to need them. Relationship starts with God, but none of us have everything that we need.

I write. I write a lot. I write six days a week on my personal blog. I love to write. Writing comes easy to me. Grammar, on the other hand, doesn't. I stink at grammar. On nearly a daily basis, my wife tells me about all the mistakes that I've made on my post. I then make corrections, hoping that the errors are corrected before too many people read the blog. I need my wife. I can proof read the mess out of something, and I still miss my own mistakes.

You Stink At Something

You might be gifted at singing, but I'm sure you stink at something else. You need someone to help you in an area in which you are weak. You might be awesome at math. I need you. If the number rises above the number of fingers that I have, I'm in trouble. Also, I can't fix things. I can't even put Legos together. Some of you reading this are ninjas at constructing things. I need you!

When your identity comes from Jesus, you realize how much you really need other people. We often fight against others who are different from us. Grammar Nazis look down at those of us who don't know the difference between your/you're. However, Grammar Nazis are also missing something. They are missing how they fit into God's plan. God's plan is that we work together. God's plan is that you be used where you're strong and lean on others where you're weak. When the Bible talks about the church, want to know how it describes it? As a body. The Bible tells us that some of us are hands, eyes, and feet. Some of you are butts. You may stink, but there is still a need for you in the body.

Now how does this fit in with, *even if you were perfect?* Great question. It fits because God thinks people are important. They aren't more important than God, but they are extremely valuable. We are so valuable, God sent His son to die for us. Now we can't truly have right relationships with others until we find our identity in Jesus. We constantly fight against humans because they don't meet our needs, hurt us with their words or actions, or we become jealous or envious of them. None of that is healthy. When we find our identity in Jesus, He gives us the ability to love others like we love ourselves. To make sure that we understand how important this is, God has wired us with a need for other people. You aren't perfect in more ways than one. It's as if God intentionally left out some of the parts that you need and gave them to other people. Together you can do more than you could ever do alone!

We've got to stop fighting with one another and start working with one another. I believe that a lot of our negativity can be stopped when we realize that we are created to help each other. You can tear someone down, but it's like looking at your hand and yelling at it because it doesn't see. True Christianity is working in unity with each other in order to honor God. When someone tears us down, it hurts because we are looking for affirmation. When you understand how God wired you, it should make you think twice about tearing down other parts of the body.

Become Part of the Solution

I once heard that we should become part of the solution, instead of part of the problem. If something needs to be fixed, you can go negative, or you can give a solution to make it better. The problem is that most people don't want a solution. Most people go negative, and all they want is affirmation. This is why we don't complain to people who could do something about the problem. We complain to our spouse about our job, but he/she can't fix anything at work. We complain to our friends about our spouse, but they can't fix the problem. We complain to other church members about the pastor, but they can't…well, I guess they can go so negative that he either leaves or gets fired, but getting rid of the pastor doesn't solve the problem. It just moves it. To truly fix a problem, you have to deal with someone who can fix it. I try not to complain to people who can't fix the problem. All that does is spread negativity. If you do that, it shows that your identity is in others. It's looking for affirmation for your cause. It's wanting others to agree that you are right and those causing you concern are stupid kaka poop poo faces. You say the phrase kaka poop poo face is childish, but so is not solving the problem. The key is to figure out a potential solution to the problem and then present it to someone who can actually do something about it.

Negativity breeds negativity. It's like a snowball that rolls down a hill and gains momentum. Because you are not perfect, because your foundation is Jesus, and because you need other people, you should not tear down others.

I had a friendship that almost didn't survive someone else's negativity. I had hung out with this person a lot, and she never got on my nerves. In fact, I had a lot of fun with her. Well, one night after a party, I saw some students hanging out who were about to leave. I walked over to say goodbye and they invited me to hang out with them. I was honored. They were cool people. They then told me to keep it on the "down-low" because they didn't want my friend to join us. I asked why, and they told me how annoying she was. I didn't end up hanging out with them that night, but what they said stuck with me. The next time I hung out with my friend, she got on my nerves. Like a cheese grater, she shredded my last nerve. I don't know if, over time, I would have discovered this person's annoying habits. What I do know is that I discovered them a lot faster after someone pointed them out. Negativity breeds negativity. We can't control what others say about us, but understanding how much we need each other should motivate us not to bash others. It should lead us to want to fix the problem.

You Weren't Meant to Live Alone

I am amazed at how alone most Christians are. Weight Watchers and AA have figured out something that most Christians miss. You can't do life alone. In Weight Watchers, they have meetings where you get together with others who struggle with weight. It's helpful. With AA you not only meet with others, but you are given a sponsor to help keep you accountable. Why? It's because on our own, we will die! We will never become who God wired us to be alone. We need each other.

Do you know that right now someone is going through the exact same struggle as you? It's true. You aren't the only one addicted to porn. You aren't the only obese person addicted to food. You aren't the only liar. You aren't the only gossip. You aren't the only person who loses your temper. You aren't the only sinner out there. One of the reasons that I know we need people is because of our sinful response to sin. Here's what I mean. When we sin, the enemy comes along and plants the seed that the best thing for us to do is to go into hiding. We feel shame, so we hide. That doesn't fix the problem. Even if we promise ourselves that we won't mess up again, without the accountability of others, we will fail— gloriously. I mean think about it. Is your struggle a one-time event? Nope! That's why it's your struggle. The answer to finding freedom is not isolation. That's a lie from the devil. The answer is repenting to God and then finding someone to help keep you accountable.

Isolation is incredibly dangerous. Left to ourselves, we can make really stupid decisions. Our minds may wander to unhealthy places. I often think about this. What is the ultimate punishment when a prison inmate misbehaves? Solitary confinement. Alone time is the worst punishment a jail can throw at someone. Why? Because we weren't meant to be alone. Do we need some alone time? YES! But, too much alone time is punishment. We need others!

"As iron sharpens iron, so one man sharpens another" (Proverbs 27:17). Who is sharpening you? Maybe a better question is who are you sharpening? Your words can bring life to someone. You can speak truth to people and totally change the trajectory of their lives. This world needs you. It needs you to understand how much others need you and how much you need others.

I hate certain jobs. I hate busywork. I hate paper work. I love to brainstorm and dream. I could sit in a meeting all day long and brainstorm solutions to problems and create new ideas. I stink at getting those ideas done. I used to think that everyone else was wired like me. Someone would offer to help me type something or complete a task that I dreamed up. I would feel really bad about them having to take this awful job. Come to find out, they actually liked what I hated. They would get done with the job and thank me for letting them do it. Do what? They liked it because they are wired differently than me. Put them in a room to meet people, and they would explode. They are the get' er done type of people. They don't want to talk or strategize. They simply want to do. I need them, and they need me.

How often have our complaints been about people simply wired differently than us? When you understand just how much you need other people and how much other people need you, it helps you filter your words.

"Do everything without complaining or arguing, so that you may become blameless and pure, children of God without fault in a crooked and depraved generation, in which you shine like stars in the universe" (Philippians 2:14-15).

You can't shine in the universe when you are complaining and arguing with other Christians. Why do we notice stars? It's because they shine! When Christians fight with one another, it's an awful reflection of our God. We are called to shine!

You are not perfect. You were wired to need others. Stop fighting against how you were created. Love others deeply. Share your life with them. Find your identity in Jesus, so that you can truly love others. Stop spreading negativity towards others and start shining for Jesus.

Chapter Five

Your Real Battle

S o we need each other. We also shouldn't be negative towards one another. Then, what do we do with people who are jerks? I mean some people are just rude to us. How are we supposed to respond to them? I think the Bible has some insight that can help with this question.

"Finally, be strong in the Lord and in his mighty power. Put on the full armor of God, so that you can take your stand against the devil's schemes" (Ephesians 6:11).

You want to know what war tactics I think are really stupid? Whenever I watch a movie like the *Patriot,* I see two opposing armies lined up against each other and then they just open fire. I'm talking about Revolutionary War and the Civil War. Those jokers aren't hiding behind anything! They just stand there and hope to not get hit by a bullet. Now, if you are in the back rows, you are somewhat safe. However, if you are in the front row, you are pretty much pulling a Bon Jovi and going down in a Blaze of Glory. I mean this is the stupidest way to fight a war. The Bible says that we have a spiritual enemy known as the Devil. I personally wish there was more information about the Devil. I'd like to have a whole war manual on how to whip up on our enemy. Instead, we only have a few verses. Just because there aren't a lot of verses, doesn't mean that this stuff isn't important. First off when this author talks about our spiritual enemy, he puts it into war terms. We are in a battle. Second, we are fighting against an enemy who is scheming. This isn't an enemy that we line up against, look at, and then fire our weapon. This isn't a dumb enemy that fights us as if this is the Civil War. This is a scheming enemy who sneak attacks us. Now to make matters worse, most of us don't put on our armor to protect ourselves. Most of us live our lives only focused on the physical world. We don't prepare for battle, so we get attacked all day long by a scheming enemy and wonder why we don't have more personal victories.

Our Real Struggle Revealed

"For our struggle is not against flesh and blood, but against the rulers, against the authorities, against the powers of this dark world and against the spiritual forces of evil in the heavenly realms" (Ephesians 6:12).

Okay, now this is where it really becomes extra "schemy". The author of this verse says that our struggle is not against flesh and blood, but against the spiritual forces of evil in the heavenly realms. That's HUGE! Most of us are focused on what we can see. We've been tricked into thinking that our battle is against flesh and blood. We spend all of our time fighting against people. We have an enemy that we ignore and that we don't suit up to fight. In addition, he's got us distracted by fighting against the wrong enemy. We fight against things that we can see when we should be paying a lot more attention to things that we can't see.

I recently got attacked by some people. It wasn't easy to see that something spiritual was going on, but eventually, it became very evident. It started when I got a Facebook message that said,

> The Lord chose you to be a leader of people. To seek His face, and to find him through prayer, fasting, and worship. He has chosen you. But do you know how you are perceived? See, I know what your heart is... I know what you really mean.... BUT... you are seen as trendy, and at the moment... YUP... Easter Rocks but how many have been brought into the kingdom in the sake of comfortable small (non guided) groups and coffee? Peace!

Okay, I didn't see this as a spiritual attack. I just saw it as someone speaking a little bit of nonsense. I think they were saying that I'm part of a trendy church and not giving people the Bible. It didn't make sense because "Easter Rocks" was another church's Easter slogan, and at the time, my church didn't have small groups. Well, that same week I did a blog post on naked zombies. It was supposed to be a funny post, and the vast majority of people understood that. The same day that I get the Facebook message about Next Level Church, I then get this email about my blog post, "Sorry Rob, this was in poor taste, with no redeeming value. Check with Monica next time."

Now, I think it was because I had already received one negative message for that day, but I decided to respond to this email. I let the person know that I try to do random funny posts to connect with people. There are a lot of people who faithfully read my blog who don't know Jesus. My hope is to keep them interested with the funny posts, so they will stick around for the Jesus posts. I also told him that Monica read the blog and thought it was funny. I then asked that he please keep negative comments to himself. He didn't like my response. In fact, he went on to say that a pastor should never respond the way that I responded to him. He said that he's trying to look out for me because this blog post could cause some to not want to come to our church. The crazy thing is that I never cussed at the guy, used excessive exclamation points, or attacked him. I tried to reply in a respectful way and I got accused of being a jerk. At this point, I was starting to get a little rattled. I had wasted time trying to respond personally to a message that was sent from someone I didn't know. After multiple emails back and forth, I finally just let it drop. A little while later, I get two more negative comments. This time, one of them simply said that I was stupid. Okay, it doesn't stop there. This same week I did a follow up blog post apologizing for offending anyone with my zombie post. On that post, the Facebook person came back and submitted this comment on my blog,

"Honestly…. I have read every blog post and article. Your church is amazing with it's community and social groups. BUT… there is no meat. There is just milk. PUSH your congregations to PUSH the gospel out into the world. What a great community mind set BUT PUSH it out! Thanks brother!"

Okay, now this time they were saying that I don't give my church the meat of the Bible. This person has never been to our church and I don't know him, personally. Now after wasting time worrying about the first two negative messages, I started to get suspicious that there was more going on than I could see. When I saw the next two negative comments, I didn't get angry. I recognized that my enemy is not "flesh and blood". Now, why did I show you those negative comments? Well, it's so you know that if you send negative comments my way, I will publish them in a book for the world to see. I kid, I kid. I put them there so you could see what I learned. I stopped focusing on the world that I could see and allowed God to change my perspective. By the time I got the fifth comment, I was able to completely dismiss it.

Your Battle

Now, this week you might not have been bombarded by negative emails, Facebook messages, or blog comments, but I wonder what has taken your focus off of the enemy? Maybe, for you, it's been a rebellious kid. Or, maybe for you, it's been a jerk of a boss. Or, maybe for you, it's been someone who hasn't given you the attention that you think you deserve. I don't know what has taken your attention away from the real enemy, but I bet there has been something. Maybe, for you, instead of focusing on the enemy, you have been focusing on the problem. The point is that if the Devil can get you fighting against something else, then he knows you won't have time to mess with him. While we are dealing with the worries of this world, Satan is having his way with us. We are fighting against an enemy that we can't see. We are fighting against an enemy that has "schemy" ways. He'll do anything he can to keep us away from the presence of God. The problem is that while he's beating us up, we don't even know it's him because we are focused on the things that we can see, instead of the things that we can't see.

I hope that this scares some of you into action. A spiritual being affects us. We think we are just grumpy. Maybe we are just grumpy, or maybe there is a spiritual force out there that is tearing us down. Your spouse is getting on your nerves; well maybe he/she is a jerk, or maybe there is a spiritual being out there that wants you focused on him/her being a jerk instead of focused on begging God for your spouse to fall in love with Jesus. You receive a negative comment. Maybe the person needs to have fire fall down from Heaven and destroy him or maybe he needs some grace. You might be getting scared because you are thinking that this is like some horror movie. You hear spiritual war, and you think *The Ring* or *Exorcist*. We should fear this enough to do something about it, but we shouldn't be afraid. In fact, look at what the Bible says, "Submit yourselves, then, to

God. Resist the devil, and he will flee from you" (James 4:7). Okay, did you catch that? We can actually resist the Devil, and when we do, he will flee. This chapter shouldn't leave any of you in fear. It should cause you to rise up. We can resist the Devil, and he will get ADD and leave us alone. Squirrel. Get it? People often joke that ADD people get distracted by squirrels.

You Ain't So Bad!

I don't know how you feel about Rocky movies, but I love them! One of my favorites is Rocky III. If you haven't seen Rocky III, then you need to know it's awesome. Rocky fights this big bad fighter named Clubber Lang, and Rocky gets badly beaten. He becomes afraid. However, the movie ends with Rocky fighting Lang one more time, and this time he's not afraid. This fight is glorious. Rocky starts talking junk to Clubber Lang. He gets hit and says, "You ain't so bad. You ain't so bad. You ain't nothing!" I love it! I love how Rocky stands his ground. As Christians, we need to be looking at our enemy and saying, "You ain't so bad. You ain't so bad. You ain't nothing!" I'm not afraid of the Devil because we've got God on our side. The Devil is not God's equal. God is all powerful, and the Devil is not. So when we get attacked, we can resist and trust God that the Devil ain't so bad. He's going to get ADD (SQUIRREL) and leave us alone when we resist. The problem is that most of us aren't focused on him. Most of us are focused on the physical world, and we think that's our problem. However, our battle isn't against the physical world. It's against a spiritual world that we can't see. So when you are feeling attacked, when you are feeling worried, when you are getting upset at the physical world, then you need to see this is an attempt to beat you up. This is war! Now the author goes on to tell us how we can fight back against this spiritual world. He goes on to tell us what we can do about it. Look at what he says next,

Therefore, put on the full armor of God, so that when the day of evil comes, you may be able to stand your ground, and after you have done everything, to stand. Stand firm then, with the belt of truth buckled around your waist, with the breastplate of righteousness in place, and with your feet fitted with the readiness that comes from the gospel of peace. In addition to all this, take up the shield of faith, with which you can extinguish all the flaming arrows of the evil one. Take the helmet of salvation and the sword of the Spirit, which is the word of God (Ephesians 6:13-16).

The author doesn't give us a lot of commentary on our defenses. He says that we need to stand our ground. That's what we are doing now. We are standing our ground. We aren't going to be moved. We are going to make God a priority. We are going to stand. Next, he says that we have the belt of truth buckled around our waist. Now, this is important because the Devil is a liar. "He's a liar, liar, pants on fire". That joker is nothing but a bag of lies. The Bible says,

"He was a murderer from the beginning, not holding to the truth, for there is no truth in him. When he lies, he speaks his native language, for he is a liar and the father of lies" (John 8:44b).

This is HUGE! A spiritual force that lies to us with devious lies that are not easy to detect attacks us. The only way that we can detect them is if we have the Bible all up in our lives.

I Never Understood, "Get Behind Me Satan"…
Until Now

There is a conversation that Jesus has with His disciples that used to always throw me for a loop. I could never understand Jesus' response until I put it in this context. Look at this conversation that Jesus has with His disciples.

From that time on, Jesus began to explain to his disciples that he must go to Jerusalem and suffer many things at the hands of the elders, the chief priests and the teachers of the law, and that he must be killed and on the third day be raised to life. Peter took him aside and began to rebuke him. "Never, Lord!" he said. "This shall never happen to you!" Jesus turned and said to Peter, "Get behind me, Satan! You are a stumbling block to me; you do not have in mind the concerns of God, but merely human concerns. (Matthew 16:21-23).

Now stick with me on this one. Jesus tells his closest followers that He's going to have to die for their sins. Out of love, Peter says, "Not on my watch." Peter, because he loves Jesus, says, "I'm not going to let them kill you." Now that seems like a great response to me. In fact, I would think that Jesus would respond by saying, "Thanks Peter for having my back. You are the man." However, Jesus doesn't respond that way. Jesus says, "Get behind me, Satan!" He calls Peter, "Satan". How many counseling sessions did Peter have to go through after that insult? As I said, this never made sense to me until I put it into the context of what we are talking about. Jesus knew the Bible so well that He could sense a lie even when it was disguised as love. Jesus knew His enemy wasn't flesh and blood, but that even well meaning people who love us can be used by the Devil. We have to be committed to truth. So someone sends me an email that makes me start second guessing what we are doing at Next Level Church. Someone sends me a Facebook message that makes me start second-guessing if I'm even listening to God. It came from other Christians—well- meaning Christians. Now I can either waste my time fighting against them, or I can stand on the truth. Let me ask you a question. What person has you distracted this week? What person is Satan using to distract you from what God wants to do you in your life? Is it your spouse? Your enemy is not your spouse. Is it your kids? Your enemy is not your kids. Maybe it's not even a person, but it's just a lie. Is it the lie that you aren't good enough? Is it the lie that you'll never over come your temptations? Is it a lie that you have to hide your sin, and you can't confess it to someone else? Is it a lie that God can't use you because you've messed up so much? We have to stand our ground and be committed to the truth—the truth of the Bible. Jesus says, "We shall know the truth, and the truth will set us free." Many struggles that we face are because we've believed a lie. Satan twists things to lie to us. The only way that we are going to be able to untangle ourselves is to face the truth. So before I leave this part of the armor, I just want to challenge you to think about what your struggle is. Whatever your struggle is, do some analytical thinking and figure out what the lie is. Then go to biblegateway.com and type in the keyword to search for whatever the truth is to your lie. Find some truth. Battle against the lie. Stand your ground. After discovering the truth, Paul tells us take up the shield of faith and the helmet of salvation. The shield of faith believes that God is who He says He is. It believes that even though we can't see God, He's on our side. He's fighting for us. He's given us everything that we need to overcome our enemy. Then, we must protect our mind with the helmet of salvation. Salvation comes from Jesus, and Paul makes it clear that when you become saved your life is different. You put away your old life and strive to live a new life that resembles the One who saved you. Let's look at it one more time,

"Take the helmet of salvation and the sword of the Spirit, which is the word of God" (Ephesian 6:16).

Notice, everything else about our armor is defensive. That is, it's all here to protect us. The only thing that is offensive is the sword of the Spirit, which Paul says is the word of God. The word of God is so important to us because it's our only weapon. If you don't know the Bible, you can't fight back against your enemy. If you don't know the

Bible, then you will continue to be pulled down by the physical world and the things that you can see. If you don't know the Bible, your life may be controlled by drama, stress, worry, and temptation. If you don't know the Bible then you can't find true freedom in Jesus. The Bible is our sword! If we are going to win this battle, then we have to read the Bible, think about it, talk about it, memorize it, and then do it all over again. This is war! I don't know about you, but I ain't going out without a fight. When Satan attacks me, I'm gonna knock him out, "Mamma said, 'Knock you out'." Most churches turn into churches that are filled with negativity. I think it's because even well- meaning Christians forget that their words can be used by the Devil. Let's be known by our love for each other. Let's be known by our love for others who are not like us. Let's be known for loving Jesus passionately, loving others passionately, and always making a practical difference in the world, in Jesus' name. Let's remember that our battle is not against flesh and blood!

Chapter Six

Flip the Script

Negativity is everywhere. We don't often think twice about tearing someone down, but we do think twice about giving someone a compliment. Why is that? We say things like "I wouldn't want their head to get big." So even when we do give a compliment, it often comes with a negative slant. Here are some common things that I've heard after I've delivered a sermon.

- "You were actually funny today." Why throw in "actually"? It implies that I'm not normally funny.
- A guy once said to me when I was on staff at a church and not the primary speaker, "I don't normally like it when you speak, but today was good."
- "That was a great talk. It wasn't the best ever. I wouldn't want you to get a big head."

I normally don't let such comments get to me. I smile and nod and then laugh about the comments with my wife. I know that God uses my talks. I try not to preach for man's approval, anyway. It just always strikes me as interesting how people feel like they have to be careful in their compliments. They wouldn't want to encourage someone so much that his head swells.

When You Think Something Nice...Say It

I once heard a pastor say that if we think something nice, we should say it. That has stuck with me. If you ever think something nice, you should say it without hesitation. If you think something nice, you should text it, tweet it, Facebook it, blog about it, or go old school and pick up the phone and call someone to tell them your nice thought. Let's shower people with encouraging words. Our world is negative. It's really negative. Instead of adding to the negativity, let's encourage those around us. Let's not hesitate to say good things, but think twice before we say something negative.

Keeping Track of Your Negative

Keeping track of things is hard to do. I know. I've tried to keep track of calories, money, how many times I've jogged, and girlfriends. Lucky for me, I've only had one girlfriend because I stink with numbers and keeping track. Now stick with me on this one.

Even though it's hard to keep track, it's crucial. Keeping track of calories lets me know how much food I've actually eaten. Keeping track of my money lets me know where I'm spending it, and it helps me know how to budget. Keeping track of the miles I've jogged helps me know when I need to buy new jogging shoes. Keeping track of girlfriends is important if you're dating two at once, but that's just wrong. If you have to count your girlfriends, then you should stop reading this and break-up with all but one. Seriously, this doesn't end well.

I'm not done. If you are dating more than one girl then you will end up being taken down town to Chinatown. If you live in a place without a Chinatown, you'll be taken down to No.1 Chinese restaurant. It sounds good, but have you ever heard of Chinese torture? Google it. I digress. Now I'm done.

What does all this have to do with being negative? I'm glad you asked. I want you to keep track of your negativity. How many times do you go negative in a day?

When I count calories and then add them up at the end of the day, I am shocked at how much I consume. I wonder if the same thing would be true if we kept up with our negative words?

Now I don't just want you to keep track of the negative things that you are thinking or about to say. I want you to replace whatever negative thing you are about to say with something positive. So seriously, grab a notepad and keep track of your negativity so you can reflect on it at the end of the day.

I know someone who calls a famous actress "stroke face." This person really doesn't like her acting. Now, you don't have to like this actresses' movie. You don't have to see them. At the same time you can flip the script, and find something positive in the actress. Maybe for you, it's not an actor. Let's keep going with this. You see someone wearing an ugly outfit, and you say, "Man looks at the outside, but God looks at the heart." Or, you are about to go negative on sparkling vampires from Twilight, but you say, "Thanks to them, I no longer have to get a tan at the beach. I can be pale and chicks will dig it. Thanks Emo Vampires!" You get the point?

We've got to flip the script. Christians need to set the example with their words. Christians should think twice about the negative things that they say and not hesitate to say something positive.

Words are Like Atomic Bombs

One of the biggest lies I've ever heard is "Sticks and stones will break your bones, but words will never hurt you." Do what? Words hurt! Bones heal. A wicked word can stick with us for years. If sticks and stones break our bones, then words are like Atomic Bombs that utterly destroy us. A negative word bomb can ruin your day, your night's sleep, your understanding of God's view of you, and has the potential to shape you into something that doesn't reflect Jesus.

Some people have said things to me that made me wish they had used sticks or stones, instead of words. When I was a little kid, we went to visit my grandpa. My grandpa was from a different time. He fought in World War I. He was fifty years old when my dad was born. He was in his 80s when this encounter happened. I don't remember who else was there, but I remember it being all kids and Grandpa. He lived on a farm and took us for rides on his tractor. In order to get to the tractor, we had to shimmy under a barbed wire fence. As I started to crawl under it, my grandpa made a joke about me not fitting because I was fat. I wasn't a fat kid. I wasn't crack skinny, but I didn't have a muffin top. Those careless words stuck with me. I'm not blaming my grandpa for making me fat, today. I blame a slow metabolism and vegetables for tasting gag nasty. If vegetables tasted better, I'd eat a lot more of them. I kid, I kid. I don't blame anyone for my weight; however, there is something inside of me that refuses to be skinny. I've run a half marathon. I exercise multiple times a week. I even attempt to lose weight the right way. Whenever I get to a certain weight, something kicks in with my brain, and I put weight back on. It's mental. It's also spiritual. My temptation in life is food. I can't go to a party and hang out at the food table, or I will leave feeling gag nasty because I've eaten way too much. I love food, but I also believe that I'm fat. It's the way that I view myself. The way that you view yourself becomes your reality. Words are powerful.

Maybe you view yourself as negative. You've got to flip the script. Don't you dare say out loud to someone, "I'm just a negative person." Maybe you view yourself as inferior to others. Maybe you view yourself as dumb, or lazy, or unlovable. Flip the script. You see people have said things to you that stuck with you. Their words helped shape your identity, but your identity is no longer in their words! Your identity is in the King of Kings. Just as our identity has been shaped by others, the sad truth is that our words have also negatively shaped others. You can't control other people's words, but you can control what you say. If you think something nice, say it. Help people become who God wired them to be.

I Almost didn't do what God Called Me to do

One of the hardest decisions that I've ever made was to start a church. One of the reasons it was hard was because of some words that someone spoke over me. You see, I was scared to start a church for various reasons. I was scared because my wife had just given birth to twins. I was scared because I didn't know how insurance would get paid. I was scared because I didn't want to fail. I knew God was leading me, but my fears paralyzed me from taking action. I finally got to the point where my conviction outweighed my fear. I was being disobedient by not doing what God was leading me to do. So, my first step was to talk to someone close to me. Well, it was actually my second step. Talking to my wife was the first step. My wife was on board and fully supportive. After my wife, I needed to talk to one friend. This person didn't have the power to stop what God was telling me to do, but could make life really hard. I prayed so hard for God's favor over that conversation. I literally cried out to God and asked Him to give me favor with this person. The conversation didn't go the exact way that I wanted it to go. The bottom line was that this person felt strongly that I couldn't plant a church. I was actually excited that he couldn't imagine me doing this. I told him that the Bible is filled with stories of men and women who didn't have the gifts or talents, yet God used them anyway. I wasn't planting a church to become famous. I didn't seek this out. I felt like God was leading me to do this. Words are powerful! This person was not interested to hear what God was telling me. Words were said. Hurtful words. In fact, I delayed planting a church for four months because of this person's words. At one point, I even said that the door was 99% closed. I felt God was calling me, but I didn't want to be stupid and ignore this person's words. I knew that if God was calling me, potentially, He might be calling me to wait. So for the next few months, I prayed. I prayed a lot. I even applied for multiple jobs at other churches. I never got a peace about anything. In fact, I felt a weight of sadness. How could what I felt like God was leading me to do be the complete opposite of what this valued friend thought?

Now, contrast this with a conversation that I had almost four months later. I felt like God was leading me to talk to someone whom I only kind of know. His name is Ben Arment. He's a dreamer, author, and full of awesome. Ben's blog is read by bazillions of people. His influence is legendary. He has the cell phone numbers of all of my pastor heroes. You know how if you play sports, you look up to certain athletes and model your game after them. Well, there are certain pastors that I respect a great deal, and Ben knows them. I tell you that just to say he's someone with influence. I didn't know if he'd have time to meet with me. He lives about 45 minutes away. I sent him a message on Twitter and waited to hear back. I think this was a God thing because not only did he have time, but he asked if I needed to talk just to him, or if this should be a connecting lunch. He's a master connector. He told me that for some reason he had a sense that I needed to talk to him, without others. I confirmed, and we scheduled a lunch. During that lunch, Ben poured encouragement over me. I told him that I felt like the best gift that God had given me was my speaking ability. I then told him that I don't think I'm the best speaker ever, but that it's the best gift I have. Ben interrupted my thought and said, "You are a great speaker." He then told me that I cut myself short. I don't have a fat clue how he's heard me speak. To this day, I don't know how he knows what he knows about me, but he said it with passion and conviction. Over the next 45 minutes, Ben spoke encouraging words over me. In fact, when I told him I was afraid to do this because of money, he said that if I got in a bind to call him, and he'd help support me financially. He said he didn't think I'd have a problem raising the funds to start a church. He told me that he thought it was what God was calling me to do. I left that lunch, and I sat in the parking lot of Panera crying. These were not tears of sadness. My sadness was gone. This was relief. Maybe I wasn't crazy for believing that God was calling me to do this. Maybe this risk would be the greatest adventure of my life. Shoot, I couldn't even say, "maybe" while sitting in that parking lot. Before I drove back home, I knew that God was calling me to plant a church. A month later, a new church was born.

I'm not suggesting that we lie to people. If we don't believe in them or we have words of caution, we should share them in a loving way. There is more on this in the next chapter. At the same time, I think the advice my mom always gave me is timeless, "If you can't say something nice, don't say anything at all." For me, that means that if I have to engage in a hard conversation, I'm going to start by saying something nice. I'm going to build people up, so they know that I believe in them. I will then share the truth in love, but not before they know the good things I see God doing in their life. The point is that our words have the potential to build someone up or tear someone down. We need to be very careful with words. What if our words hinder someone from fulfilling a dream? What if our words inspire others to be better than they ever thought they could be?

I don't know about you, but I want people to soar. I want people to hear my words and fall more in love with Jesus. I want people to hear my words and know that all things are possible with God. I want people to hear my words and become better because of them. Think about this. When God created things, how did He do it? He spoke things into existence. He gave life to things by simply saying words. The Bible says that we are created in the image of God. Maybe that's why our words are so powerful. Maybe that is how we have the power to speak life or death into someone.

Who is someone that you need to call right now and encourage? Is there someone in your life that you need to apologize to because you hurt them with your words? Is there a hard conversation that you need to have? Do not put it off. Speak the truth to them in love. Your words matter. They bring either life or death.

When your identity is truly in Jesus, your words should reflect Jesus. Some people may choose to hate, but you don't have to. Flip the script.

Chapter Seven

Speaking the Truth in Love— Confrontation

I am a recovering people pleaser. With that comes the scary fear of confrontation. I hate it. In fact, I used to avoid it like the plague. When someone needs to be confronted, I normally have a conversation in my head. It's amazing. I'm awesome in my own head. Everything I say is said with confidence. The offenders are left apologizing and telling me how wrong they were. I wish it were as easy outside of my head.

What used to happen is I'd have a conversation in my head, and then I'd end up convincing myself not to talk to the person in real life. I'm a chicken. My wife, on the other hand, is not afraid to speak her mind. My wife is very confident. She's not a people pleaser. Yet even with my wife's ability to speak her mind, she has a ton of friends. In fact, she has more best friends than anyone I've ever met. Observing my wife has helped me understand that sometimes people want to hear the truth. They just want to hear it in love. Ephesians 4:11-15 says,

> It was he who gave some to be apostles, some to be prophets, some to be evangelists, and some to be pastors and teachers, to prepare God's people for works of service, so that the body of Christ may be built up until we all reach unity in the faith and in the knowledge of the Son of God and become mature, attaining to the whole measure of the fullness of Christ. Then we will no longer be infants, tossed back and forth by the waves, and blown here and there by every wind of teaching and by the cunning and craftiness of men in their deceitful scheming. Instead, **speaking the truth in love,** we will in all things grow up into him who is the Head, that is, Christ. From him the whole body, joined and held together by every supporting ligament, grows and builds itself up in love, as each part does its work (bold emphasis mine).

This verse is loaded. First, it says that God has gifted some of us in roles that should prepare others for ministry—pastors and teachers. It's the idea of the body of Christ. It goes with the discussion in Chapter Four. People with these gifts are supposed to equip the church so that believers won't be infants in their faith. From there, the author says that we are to speak the truth in love. What's a sign of a mature believer according to that verse? Speaking the truth in love. Sometimes, we need to confront someone. Sometimes, people need to hear the truth. The problem is that when we deliver truth, it's sometimes wrapped in harsh words and attitudes of rejection.

Not too long ago, I was inspired to write a blog post. It had to do with homosexuality and the polarizing views that this topic brings out in people. I want to share that post here because I think it makes my point.

Why I Have Homosexual Friends

There is nothing more polarizing in America today than a person's view on homosexuality. Men in deep V-neck shirts and skinny jeans, people who like Moe's more than Chipotle, whether Tiger Woods can dunk a basketball, adults knowing every word to the song "Call Me Maybe", and whether Dirk Nowitzki counts as a great white basketball player because he is not from America are all distant polarizing topics. That last one is a real conversation that I had. Someone told me that there were no good white NBA players. When I said Dirk, they told me he didn't count because he was from Germany. I digress.

Recently, I watched on Facebook as people filled their statuses with either their displeasure or pleasure over a vote in North Carolina. It was hard for me to get on Facebook that day. It was sad. Nobody was being persuaded one way or another. It was just people venting because they felt defeated or people gloating because they felt victorious.

I believe that homosexuality is a sin, but I also believe that the way a lot of Christians treat the subject is sin as well. I have friends who are homosexuals. Some of them struggle with this decision, and some of them don't. I know all of them know my beliefs. So, how are we still friends?

Stick with me on this one. I have friends who are Democrats, and I have friends who are Republicans. I'm what I'd call Idon'tgivearipaboutpolitics-ican. I have friends who believe in infant baptism even though they know that I am a Baptist and don't. I have friends who don't like Chipotle. I have friends who love the Celtics. Being a Lakers fan, that's not easy. I have friends who say they are Christians and believe that the Bible's views on premarital sex are outdated and no longer apply. I was a virgin until my wedding night.

So how do I do it? Respect.

I respect people. People matter to God. Even if their views differ from mine, they still have value.

If Christians put themselves in the shoes of a homosexual, I think they would have a lot of empathy. It can't be easy to feel unwelcome in some places. It's not easy having messages preached against you. It's not easy having feelings of love towards someone and being told that it's sin. It's not easy to be made fun of.

People rarely change their lives because they are yelled at. In fact, in this day and age, people don't even want to say "Hello" to you until you've won them over. When someone knows that you care about them, and not just their beliefs, they may put up with your differences. You can tell people to go and sin no more, but they won't listen until they know you love them.

Remember the story of Jesus and the woman caught in adultery. It's where we get the line "Let him who is without sin, cast the first stone" (John 8:7). Jesus saves the woman's life by convicting her accusers. One by one, the men who condemned her dropped their stones. Jesus won the woman over, and then said, "Go and sin no more." Christians today often say, "Sin no more, and then we can have a relationship."

Whenever we preach against a sin, we should have great empathy towards those who live with it. Whether it's worry, over- eating, lying, addiction, looking at nudie girls, apathy, alcoholism, etc. our hearts should break for the people we are talking about.

Even if they don't agree that what they are dealing with is sin, our hearts should still break. If our hearts don't break, it's a sign that we are blind to our own sin. At the end of the day, we all choose something over Jesus. That's sin! Thank God for grace and forgiveness. It's not like I don't sin daily. I don't want to. I strive to live for God, but I'm not perfect. It just so happens that my sin is still welcome in the church.

This subject has been on my mind a lot lately. I've been afraid to write about it because it has the potential to tick off both sides. Some will say that I'm not harsh enough. Some will say that I'm too harsh. I would say that I'm trying to love people to Jesus.

Learning When to Say Something

Whether it's sin, or just someone who needs confrontation, we should have the courage to speak the truth…in love. There are two questions that I ask myself whenever I start having one of those conversations in my head.

1. Have I ever communicated my expectation with the person?
2. Is my expectation realistic?

Before I confront someone, I want to make sure that I've made my expectations clear. I shouldn't get angry at people who don't know my expectations. For example, not too long ago, there was a guy who would get up during our service and walk out a side door of the auditorium. It was annoying. Even more than that, it was distracting. Everyone would turn to see him leave. Then he would come back in that same door. Now in my mind common sense says, "Don't walk out a door in the middle of a service to distract everyone." Newsflash: What's common sense to one person, may not be common sense to others. The point is, I had an expectation that was never communicated. So my approach was to speak the truth in a loving manner. I simply asked the guy to no longer use that door, and I told him why. Guess what? He punched me in the face and never came back to our church. I kid, I kid. You have lots of situations where you've become angry, but you've never made your expectations clear. Before you jump down a person's throat, take a deep breath, calm down, and then have a conversation to reveal your expectations.

Now some expectations are unrealistic. It's unrealistic for my wife to think that I'm going to be able to fix things like her dad. Her dad is a mechanical ninja. I have to read the instructions to make Kool-Aid. I'm just not gifted that way. So for Monica to get upset with my lack of construction ability wouldn't make sense. I'm not wired or gifted to fix things like her dad. She has to change her expectations. Now, this one is huge! As a Christian, I have an expectation that other Christians will live a certain way. Sometimes, Christians put that expectation on those who don't believe. When I was in middle school, the church denomination that I was a part of led a boycott on Disney. I think it was because Disney gave health benefits to homosexuals, or had a gay parade. Now, here's the problem with that. It was an unrealistic expectation. It's unrealistic for non-Christians to be held to the same standards as Christians. Plus, Disney is one of the few family friendly companies out there. It made my denomination stand out for all the wrong reasons. It made Christians in this denomination rebel against their own denomination because, you had better believe, we were not going to miss watching *Aladdin* in the theaters. I was a full-blown rebel with a cause. I saw *Aladdin* five times in the theaters. "A whole new world. Don't you dare close your eyes…" Okay, Aladdin was not even out during the boycott, but you get the point. The point is that sometimes we need to speak the truth in love, but before we do, we need to figure out if we have ever expressed our expectations and if our expectations are realistic.

One More Test

Depending on how you answer those two questions, it may be time to confront someone. Before you do, make sure that what you are sharing is biblically based and not just your opinion. An example might be when someone is doing something illegal but doesn't feel it's wrong. I've sometimes dealt with that when leading teenagers who smoke pot. Now my expectation is that a Christian shouldn't smoke pot, but teens say things like, "If God grew it, then it can't be bad." Well, God also grew poison ivy, so why don't you smoke that? I have often had conversations where I have shared my expectations with students. I don't feel like my expectations are unrealistic, and I've had to confront students with the truth of the Bible. The truth is, the Bible doesn't say, "Don't smoke pot." It does, however, talk about not getting drunk. Those verses can apply to smoking pot. When that doesn't work, I go to Paul's trusty verse that is a catch all. Paul says, "Everything is permissible for me—but not everything is beneficial. Everything is permissible for me—but I will not be mastered by anything." (I Corinthians 6:12). As a Christian, we have freedom in Christ, but that doesn't mean that we should abuse that freedom. Paul says that we should not be mastered by anything., Even when smoking pot becomes legal in the U.S., it's not a good master. I have had this exact conversation with several people. It wasn't easy. I'm still friends with them. Some of them still smoke pot on a regular basis. I spoke the truth in love, and our relationship is still intact, even though they haven't changed…yet

But for Real…What if they get Angry?

If you are like me, you are saying, "But what if they get angry at me?" Here's something that has helped me. The Bible tells us to speak the truth in love. We aren't responsible for how someone responds. We are only responsible to speak in love.

There is another issue that came up a lot while I was working with students. It wasn't easy for me to talk about it because I knew my view wasn't popular. Not only was it not popular with students, but it wasn't popular with some of the leaders. We should back up what we say with the truth in the Bible. For example, when some of the students at my church were stealing music illegally on the internet, I lovingly let them know why it was wrong. They told me that it was easy to get, so it couldn't be wrong. Stealing is stealing, no matter how easy it is. I asked them if they saw a new Dodge Charger (motor running with the keys in it, and no one was around) would it be wrong to get in and drive it home? They didn't like my example. However, I was able to have a conversation with them and show them why (even if it was easy) it was still stealing. Some agreed and stopped downloading music, illegally. Others thought I was being legalistic and kept on doing it. I didn't stop respecting the students who didn't listen to me. I simply spoke the truth in love and left the details up to God. Some people didn't like my view. Some people got angry. As their pastor, I felt like God was leading me to share a conviction birthed out of my understanding of the Bible. I had some heated debates, but because I still respected the people, our relationship continued.

Here's the bottom line; we need each other to grow. We need wise people to speak truth into our lives. We should have the confidence to confront because our identity isn't in other people. It's in Jesus. If what we are going to say is going to make someone more like Jesus, then we should say it in a loving way. We aren't responsible for how people receive things. We are only responsible to speak the truth in love. If someone gets angry or hurt, we do whatever we can to make the relationship better. Maybe it means we don't bring this up again until they are ready to talk. DON'T force an opinion on someone. Share your thoughts and then keep loving them whether or not they agree. Maybe it means they weren't ready to receive it. Maybe it means we need to spend time praying and asking God to show them the truth. It's sad to me how many Christian relationships are broken because of careless, unkind words. Let's speak the truth in love.

Chapter Eight

Forgiven People Forgive

Words can wound. In fact, some of you reading this right now are bitter towards someone who hurt you with words. The truth is that this person has power over you. Your identity is wounded. You don't need to get back. You don't need vengeance. You need to forgive.

One of my all time favorite movies is *Teenage Mutant Ninja Turtles*. I'm not a big fan of the sequels, but I love the first movie. I think it's funny, has great action, and has really cool characters. When I was a middle school student, I saw this movie multiple times in the theaters. I bought it on VHS and when DVD's took over, I purchased a copy. I haven't bought it on Blue Ray, but that's next. I've seen this movie a lot of times and out of all the scenes, there is one that stands out to me. Some of you weren't blessed to watch this movie as a kid, and others of you don't remember movies after you see them, so let me tell you about this scene. Michelangelo (the orange masked turtle) is waiting for a pizza delivery. The delivery man can't find the location because it's 122 and 8th, in a sewer. Once he finds the location, Michelangelo offers $10 when the tab was $13. The pizza delivery guy calls Michelangelo out on it, and my favorite turtle replies, "Wise man once say, forgiveness is divine, but never pay full price for late pizza." Forgiveness is divine, but I think most of us feel the same way as Michelangelo. It's a divine thing. We want people to forgive us, but when certain lines are crossed, we won't forgive them.

I'm probably the only one who struggles with forgiving others. I'm probably the only one who holds onto grudges. I'm probably the only one who has amazing and dominating arguments with people in my head. I mentioned this earlier in the book, but when someone hurts me, I wreck them in my mind. I have this confrontation with them where everything I say is acknowledged with "That's amazing, and you are right." While writing this chapter, I experienced this. I was getting tired, and I needed a little pick me up. I'm trying not to drink caffeine, so I decided to take a little break and go to Tropical Smoothie. On my way out, I asked Monica if she wanted anything. Since Starbucks is next to Tropical Smoothie, she said she would like a light caramel frappuccino. I go get my smoothie and then head over to Starbucks. As I enter, there is a huge line of people coming towards the opposite door. So I put on my afterburners and speed walk through my door to the front of the line. After the girl in front of me orders, the Starbucks barista goes to work on a drink and then comes back to a different register. I'm standing there waiting for her and then I hear this guy who was clearly in line after me say he wants an egg salad sandwich and four macchiatos. Are you kidding me!? First, egg salad sandwiches are gag nasty. Second, I was clearly first in line. Now this upset me because I was in a hurry, and now I have to wait for the server to make four drinks before making mine. Oh and it upset me because it's just not right. I look at egg salad guy, and I start destroying him in my mind. I do such a good job that he's forever forsaken egg salad sandwiches, and he buys me the drink that I was waiting for. In my mind, that was awesome. In reality, I stared at him with the stink eye and then looked the other way when he made eye contact. Forgiveness is divine, but never cut in line before me, and order a gag nasty egg salad sandwich.

I know that I'm not the only one who struggles to forgive. In fact, I know that right now some of you are bitter towards a family member who hurt you with words. I know that some of you if you are honest with yourself, would say that you hate an ex-spouse. I know that some of you have former friends who are now no longer a part of your life because of some incident. Some of you are holding onto grudges from people who hurt you. They said something that wasn't true, or maybe they weren't there for you. In fact, I think that we all bear the scars of hurt caused by other people. I forget what my wife tells me to get at the grocery store five minutes after she tells me, but I remember every detail from incidents when people have hurt me.

Forgiveness Isn't Optional For Christians

Forgiveness for a Christian isn't optional. I want to search the Bible and explore why those who seek to follow Jesus must forgive.

"Our Father in heaven, hallowed be your name, your kingdom come, your will be done, on earth as it is in heaven. Give us today our daily bread. And forgive us our debts, as we also have forgiven our debtors. And lead us not into temptation, but deliver us from the evil one" (Matthew 6:12-13, NIV).

Okay, let's stop here for a second. This is a familiar passage of scripture. Jesus gives us a template on how we should pray. This is something that you may have grown up praying in church. For some reason a lot of football teams also pray it before they take the field. Look at the second to last part of this verse, "Forgive us our debts, as we also have forgiven our debtors". Did you catch what Jesus said? There is a link between your relationship with God and your ability to forgive those who have hurt you.

Now you might be familiar with that prayer, but the very next line is the part that has been ninja kicking me in the face. In fact, one of the reasons that I picked this verse is because I've never heard it taught before. I've heard pastors teach on the Lord's prayer, but I have never heard a single preacher teach about this next part. Look at what Jesus says,

"For if you forgive other people when they sin against you, your heavenly Father will also forgive you. But if you do not forgive others their sins, your Father will not forgive your sins" (Matthew 6:14-15).

Do what?! That's HUGE! Forgiven people forgive. If you don't forgive others, then God won't forgive you. Those are Jesus words.

I struggle with this. I struggle with this because I have been taught that God is a God of grace. I struggle with this because it feels like it puts a lot of power back on my works and me. If I do this, then God will do that. Whenever you read the Bible and come across a verse that is hard to understand, you should always compare it to other verses in the Bible. I don't believe the Bible contradicts itself. So let's jump over to what Paul, one of the major authors of the New Testament, says in Ephesians 2:8 (NIV) "For it is by grace you have been saved, through faith—and this is not from yourselves, it is the gift of God— not by works, so that no one can boast". Paul makes it clear that it is by grace that you have been saved, and it's not by works. That means that God doesn't love us because of the good things that we do.

Years ago, I invited a friend in high school to church. He said that he couldn't come because he had to get some things right in his life before he came to church. That's a typical belief. It's the thought that I have to be good and then God will love me. No! God loves you period. You can't do anything to make God love you any more than He already does. It is by grace that you have been saved, and it's not because of anything that you've done. It's only because Jesus died on a cross for you, and Jesus didn't die for good people. We all have sinned and fallen short of God (Romans 3:23). I don't know if you feel this tension, but I feel it. Jesus says that if we don't forgive people, then God won't forgive us. That sounds like works. Paul then says that it's by grace that you have been saved, and it's not by works. Well, doesn't forgiving people kind of sound like works? Let's continue in the Bible and see what else it says. This, once again, is Paul and he says, "Bear with each other and forgive one another if any of you has a grievance against someone. Forgive as the Lord forgave you" (Colossians 3:13, NIV). Okay here is the key to unlock this whole mess. The reason that Jesus can say that God won't forgive you unless you forgive others is because a true sign of a Christian is a person who has been forgiven! When we really think about all that Jesus forgave us of, it's mind blowing. How many times have you turned your back on God? How many times have you lied, cheated, lusted, or murdered someone with your thoughts because they cut in line in front of you and ordered a gag nasty egg salad sandwich? Is that last one still just me? I'm a work in progress.

Here's the point: Forgiven people forgive. You see, forgiving people doesn't change God's perspective of you. If you forgive someone, it doesn't make God love you any more than He already does. Forgiving people is a sign that you have been forgiven. If you can't forgive someone, then it's a sign that you don't understand how you have been forgiven.

Jesus is Hardcore

If you think this is a hard teaching, you should have lived in Jesus day. You see, in Jesus day the common practice was "an eye for an eye, and a tooth for a tooth". Translation: If someone hurts you, then you hurt them equally. Strange as it seems, this was a biblical idea. When God set up order with the children of Israel, He established a justice system based on "an eye for an eye". This is often hard for modern day human minds to understand. Where's the grace in this? Some may adamantly disagree with me, but my understanding is that God wanted His people to be set apart. In order to do that, He set high standards. "An eye for an eye" was to prevent people from stealing or murdering. The idea is that if the consequences are strong enough, people are more likely to resist the temptation to hurt others. That's why I didn't walk over and wipe that nasty egg salad sandwich in the face of that guy at Starbucks. I would get in serious trouble for that. Although it would have been glorious, it was not worth the consequences of going to jail for assault.

When Jesus comes on the scene, He talks about forgiveness...a lot. So much so that His disciples have a conversation with Him and one of them attempts to impress Jesus with how much he's willing to forgive. Look at what happens, "Then Peter came to Jesus and asked, 'Lord, how many times shall I forgive my brother or sister who sins against me? Up to seven times'?" (Matthew 18:21-22, NIV). Now let's stop here for a second. The common teaching from Rabbis in Jesus day was that a person was to forgive someone up to three times. If someone hurt you and asked for forgiveness it was like baseball. People were allowed three strikes and if they went over three, then you didn't have to forgive them. So Peter has been listening to Jesus' teaching, and He tries to impress Jesus. He is basically saying "Jesus I'm willing to forgive up to seven times". Now I'm not great with math but that is a little more than two times as much as what the Rabbis were teaching. Peter is probably feeling pretty good about himself, but Jesus responds with, "I tell you, not seven times, but seventy times seven". Some scholars do not believe that Jesus was being literal when he said, "seventy times seven," but that would mean that if someone hurt you 490 times, you would have to forgive 490 times. I'm thinking, "Hurt me once shame on you; hurt me 490 times, shame on me." That's a lot of times to forgive someone who has hurt you. Many scholars believe that Jesus wasn't putting a number on forgiveness, but instead, emphasizing that forgiveness is times infinity.

Then to make His point, Jesus tells a story. The story is about a king who wants to settle his accounts. He brings in a guy who owes him a huge sum of money. The debtor indicates that he can't pay, and the king then tells the guy that he and his wife and his children will be sold into slavery in order to pay off the debt. When the guy hears this, he falls to his knees and begs the king to have mercy on him. The king is full of compassion and shows this guy incredible grace. In fact, not only does the king let the man go, but he cancels the debt completely (Matt. 18:23-27). That would be unheard of in Jesus day. In our day, it's called bankruptcy, but in Jesus day this would have been a miracle. So the debtor is free to go, and then Jesus says that this man who has just been forgiven a huge debt runs into someone who owes him just a few dollars. Well the guy can't pay. You want to know what happens? The man the king set free throws his debtor in prison. The king's servants go back to tell the king, and this is where I want us to pick up,

> Then the master called the servant in. 'You wicked servant,' he said, 'I canceled all that debt of yours because you begged me to. Shouldn't you have had mercy on your fellow servant just as I had on you?' In anger his master handed him over to the jailers to be tortured, until he should pay back all he owed (Matthew 18:34).

Now that's all fine and dandy but then this next part is another ninja kick from Jesus. Look at what Jesus says next…

"This is how my heavenly Father will treat each of you unless you forgive your brother or sister from your heart" (Matthew 18:35).

I don't know about you, but I don't want God to treat me like this. I don't want to have to pay back the consequences of my sin. I can't tell you how much time I'd have to pay, but this verse is saying that if you are truly a Christian, then you will be able to forgive people from your heart. You want to know how to identify a follower of Jesus? It's someone who forgives. Think about all your sins that God has forgiven! They are "gigantor." To not forgive someone for something that they've done is like a slap in the face of our King. I have learned a ton about forgiveness from watching how my wife forgives me.

My Wife Helped me Learn how to Forgive

A few years ago, Monica and I drove to the gym. During our evening drive, she said something that really ticked me off. I can't remember what it was, and I think it's funny that in the moment we get so upset about something, but later we may not even remember what it was that upset us. Well, I go to the gym, and I'm a little frustrated. When we get to the gym, I decide that I'm going to change my attitude and try to move on from whatever upset me. I ask Monica to lift weights with me, but she doesn't want to. At that moment, I should have communicated with her. Instead, I got frustrated again. I struggle with communicating my feelings, and so I went over and started lifting weights. As I'm lifting, I'm just dwelling on how upset I am. I'm getting more and more frustrated, and I finally decide that I'm going to run home to blow off some steam.

I walk over to Monica who is on the elliptical, and I put the car keys in the cup holder of her machine. I look her in the eyes, and I say, "I'm jogging home." I knew there was a good chance that she didn't hear me, but I didn't care. I chose to be childish. So, I go for a jog that was mostly a walk. My walk was great. I cooled down from being upset. I stopped having these awesome arguments in my mind where Monica apologized and made me homemade cookies.

It is about a four mile walk to my house. While I'm enjoying my little adventure, Monica is back at the YMCA. The staff starts shutting off all the lights, and Monica can't find me anywhere. She didn't hear me say that I was jogging home. In fact, she ran into a friend of ours and had him search the men's bathroom, the sauna, and the bottom of the swimming pool. At this point, Monica starts freaking out a little bit because she doesn't have a fat clue where I am. She convinces herself that I have been "man-napped". You see when you are a kid you get kidnapped but when you are a man, it's called "man-napped". I'm a man; insert grunt here. Monica calls some of our friends and asks if they've heard from me. Suddenly, there is an all out search party for Rob.

Meanwhile, I'm skipping down the road without a care in the world. Monica is getting ready to call the cops, but decides to have a friend drive her to our house to see if I'm there. She is so shaken up from this that she doesn't even drive. She has a friend drive. About a mile from my house, Monica spots me. She asks our friends to take her back to the YMCA to get her car so that she can come pick me up. I cross into our neighborhood, and I see Monica pull up. She has this look on her face like she's been through a war. Like a stupid guy, I ask, "What's wrong?" She asks what I am doing and why I didn't tell her about it. When I saw the look on her face, I felt so guilty. I knew that my little selfish act to get back at her wasn't worth it. I knew that I had hurt her way more than her comment had hurt me. I apologized so much that night that I think it got on Monica's nerves. The next morning as Monica walks out the door to go to work, she says to me, "Rob I love you. You don't have to ask me to forgive you anymore, and you don't have to buy me flowers." She kissed me goodbye and walked out the door.

My wife had hurt my fragile feelings, and I did something to try to get back at her. I hurt her feelings, and she says that she loves me and forgives me. I don't know if you've ever been forgiven for doing something really dumb, but it's humbling. For the rest of that day, all

I could think about was how much I love Monica. All I could think about was how much I don't deserve her love. Her forgiveness rocked me. That situation actually shed a new light on Jesus' forgiveness for me. I had always just assumed that God forgave me because He was God. I mess up, and then ask for forgiveness, but I don't often think about the gravity of my sin. You see in order to forgive our sins, God sent His son to die on a brutal cross. While we are skipping along in our sin, God sends out a search party led by the Holy Spirit to find us.

When God finds us, He doesn't condemn us on the spot. He shows us a grace that we just don't deserve. When you really understand that your sin is what killed Jesus, it changes you. God forgave you despite the fact that you couldn't pay Him back. God forgave you. When you realize this, you are more ready to forgive others who hurt you.

You might be holding on to some real pain. You've been hurt, and you've been hurt badly—so badly that you can't stand the thought of letting go of your pain. You feel that if you give up your pain, you will be allowing the person who hurt you to get away with what was done. Ironically, the problem with not forgiving is that it affects us way more than it affects the person who hurt us. When you are bitter at someone that person goes along living life, but you put your life on hold because you can't move on. When we don't forgive, it only hurts us, and it's a slap in the face of our King. Forgiven people forgive—not because it's easy, and not because the person who hurt us deserves it. We forgive because God first forgave us.

Putting Forgiveness to the Test

A few years ago a relative from another state came to live with my parents. When she first moved in, I could tell that something was wrong. She wasn't acting herself. However, when I tried to talk to her about it, she would just say that she was tired. How often do we mask our hurt with an excuse? After a few days, she started talking to my siblings about me and Monica. She created all sorts of lies. Apparently, I had offended her with a comment that I said in a sermon. In an attempt to be nice, Monica had sent her my sermons on CD. In one of my talks, I had jokingly said that if you haven't seen the movie *Star Wars* then you must have been raised in a cave by wolves. Well, my relative took great offense to this because she'd never seen *Star Wars*.

From this offense, she created this whole scenario about how I worked in an occult. She told my siblings how my parents liked me more than them, and how I was brainwashing people. She even tried to have my brother secretly drive her hundreds of miles back to her hometown.

Once my parents became aware of what was happening, this relative they had tried to help was on her way back to her home. However, this whole thing stung. I had been close to this relative. Monica and I had made special trips to see her. She not only said things about me that weren't true, she tried to turn my family against me. My brother is one of my best friends, and I remember thinking that if she had turned him against me, I would be crushed.

The following Christmas, I called this relative on the phone to wish her a Merry Christmas. Friends who knew about the story were shocked. This relative has never reached out to me. She's never asked me for forgiveness. She's never apologized for her words, yet I called her. I still make a point to call her. Why? Because, forgiven people forgive.

This doesn't mean that you forget what a person did to you. This doesn't mean that you allow someone to continually abuse you. If someone is causing you physical or emotional pain, you need to know that it's okay and healthy to leave. Get to safety, and then work on forgiving them. Forgiving people doesn't mean that you allow them to continue hurting you. It just means that you aren't going to hold onto their sin. You see, your sin nailed Jesus to the cross, so when someone hurts you, let Jesus handle it. Let Him take the pain. Throw it at the cross, and then move on with your life. Jesus forgave you. A sign of an authentic Christian is a person who forgives.

Shake the Dust, and Move on

Sometimes you have to just shake the dust, and move on. My mom wrote a great little book with that title. It's based on Jesus' words to his disciples. Jesus told his closest followers that if they weren't welcomed somewhere they were to shake the dust, and move on. If you've been hurt, you need to know that it is not okay. Forgiving the person is not about saying, "It's okay". It's about shaking the dust, and moving on with your life. If someone continually hurts you, then you definitely need to move on. Shake your money maker, and get out of there. Shake the dust, and move on is about forgiving people and letting go of the pain they have caused you. Lack of forgiveness will eat you alive! It's time to shake that dust, and move on.

Can Jerry Sandusky Be Forgiven?

When I write the name Jerry Sandusky, what do you think? Maybe you don't know about him. Maybe you are one of those future people I mentioned in chapter one, and too much time has passed. Well, in my time, that name brings up a lot of anger and pain. As one of the coaches for Penn State, Sandusky was arrested for sexually abusing numerous kids. Seeing Christians' reactions on Facebook inspired me to write the following blog post…

Can Jerry Sandusky be Forgiven?

Jerry Sandusky—the name alone causes people to hulk out. A coach should never have taken advantage of his position and used it to sexually abuse the kids he coached. It's disgusting. If he did that to my son, I'd want to castrate him with a spork from Taco Bell. Why a spork? Cause it's dull...

There is a part of me that hopes that his prison sentence comes with an incredibly slippery bar of soap. Everyone knows the one rule in prison life is don't drop the soap. There is a part of me that agrees when I see people spew anger towards him on Facebook and in the media. He is sick. He deserves more than prison time. Yet, there is a part of me that is sad for Sandusky. Do what?!

It makes me sad when Christians, who have been forgiven of their sins, wish the worst on Sandusky. His sin is grotesque! So is yours! So is mine! So—Is—Mine. Let that sink in.

Forgiven people forgive. However, it doesn't mean that there aren't consequences. God is the judge.

Sandusky deserves to spend the rest of his life in jail. His sin has consequences and so does ours. Ultimately, what Sandusky needs is forgiveness. He can serve time in jail for the rest of his life, but never become broken over his sin. His sin will lead him to burn in Hell. Is that what we want?

That's what he deserves, but so do we! Jesus died for the Sanduskys just as much as He died you. Forgiven people forgive. If Jesus has forgiven you, it's a sin not to forgive. Why? Because forgiven people forgive. Jesus forgave us, and it wasn't because we weren't as bad as Sandusky. He forgave us because without Him, we are just like Sandusky. Lost. Consumed with selfishness. Blinded. We all deserve a shank in the back. If it were not for the grace of God, we might be a Sandusky. Forgiven people forgive. That's all.

How to Apply this Chapter

Forgiven people forgive. That doesn't mean that it's easy. It especially doesn't mean that what others did to you is okay. It's not okay. It's also not okay for others to continually hurt you and have power over you.

Forgiveness is the only thing that will release you. When your identity is in Jesus, it means that you do what Jesus does. It means that you aim to please Him. Jesus forgave. Jesus forgave, and it doesn't mean that our sin is okay. He forgave in order that we might have life in God. Now it's your turn.

Here's how you apply this chapter:

1. If there is someone that you need to forgive, call them now and make it right. Don't wait. If you wait, you might never do it. Forgiven people forgive.
2. If you are struggling to forgive yourself, then it's a sign that you don't understand God's forgiveness. Pray that you will grasp God's forgiveness in your life. Allow His grace to consume you. Move on from your mistakes.
3. If you have hurt someone, make it right, and ask them for their forgiveness.

Forgiven people forgive. I pray that as you read this, God will give you the courage to do what's right—even if it's hard.

Chapter Nine

Back off that Ledge

This chapter is not about basketball.

In the year 2010, the NBA basketball world was set on fire. Lebron James and Chris Bosh were joining Dwayne Wade on the Miami Heat. Sportswriters went crazy. Today people focus on Lebron's statement of winning "not 5, not 6, not 7" championships, but the media was saying the same thing. I remember reading articles about how this Miami team was going to challenge Michael Jordan's Chicago Bull's record of 72 wins. Well, that first season didn't go as planned. At one point, the Miami Heat had a 8 and 7 record. They had lost three straight. You would have thought that the world was over. Sports writers were panicking. This team wasn't supposed to lose. The problem is that the NBA season equals 82 games. The Miami Heat went on to the Finals that year to face the Dallas Mavericks. When the Heat lost the Finals, the sports world jumped on the ledge once again. They treated Lebron like he was a criminal who had stolen their hopes and dreams. They talked about blowing up the team and starting over.

Most of us live out on the ledge. We panic too quickly. We rush to conclusions. We climb out the window, stand on the ledge, and threaten to jump because life is just too bad. I have been there. The media lives there. They are all too quick to jump on the ledge and declare that it's the end of the world.

When someone tells you that you have been talked about, it's easy to want to jump out onto the ledge. It's easy to want to assume the worst and get yourself worked up into a tizzy. Problems are never solved on the ledge. It's time to take a deep breath and climb back inside.

The problem is that most of the things we freak out about aren't really that big of a deal. In fact, most of the things we worry about never happen. Think about it...what was the last thing you worried about? Most of the time, there are hypothetical worries that consume us. What if she leaves? What if they don't like me? What if I lose my job? What if I fail? We create scenarios and then freak out about them. We create drama because we forget that the outcome hasn't been written.

An Out of Whack Perception

Whenever I'm on the ledge, it is a clear picture that my perception is out of whack. It shows that I'm overestimating my problem and underestimating my God. I over estimate how bad things really are or will be, and I underestimate an all-powerful being. The God who parted the Red Sea, helped a shepherd boy slay a giant, and even raised the dead is the same God who can handle our situation. What are you freaking out about? Take a deep breath, and back off that ledge.

I remember one night I was up all night tossing and turning because one of the small groups under my leadership didn't like a decision that I made. Instead of talking to me, they talked about me. Come to find out, the leaders didn't have my back. They agreed with the rest of the group. I climbed onto the ledge .I was ready to fire these volunteers. I was ready to take over the group and start leading it myself. It did not matter that this was an all girls group. I was going to lead them or I was going to ask God to call down fire from Heaven.

"Even if you were perfect, someone would crucify you" works both ways. You are not perfect. Neither is anyone else.

Come to find out, the group that was talking about me didn't make as big of a deal about it as I had heard. In fact, they barely talked about it. Once I got a chance to calm down, I talked to the leaders. They actually had my back. The group wasn't that upset. I had heard from an unreliable source. How often do we climb on a ledge because of unreliable sources?

Sometimes, people are jerks. Sometimes, people are idiots. Sometimes, what you hear isn't the truth. Give people the benefit of the doubt. Before you climb out on the ledge, take a deep breath and go to the source.

Maybe someone is out to get you, or maybe it's a misunderstanding. Before you blow up, take a deep breath. Calm down. Talk to the source, and then react like a Christian. Back off that ledge.

Pray Yourself off that Ledge

The Bible says, "Do not be anxious about anything, but in everything, by prayer and petition, with thanksgiving, present your requests to God. And the peace of God, which transcends all understanding, will guard your hearts and your minds in Christ Jesus" (Philippians 4:6-7).

Before you even consider climbing on the ledge, you should pray. Prayer is more than just asking God for things. It's going into battle. Prayer boards up the windows of our mind and protects us from climbing on ledges. The verses above promise that when we pray, "the peace of God which transcends all understanding, will guard your hearts and minds in Christ Jesus." I don't know about you, but I want a peace that transcends all understanding. Everyone else may regularly spend time out on the ledge but not me. Not you. Not anymore.

Being on the ledge is a sure sign that our identity is in something else. Whatever we panic about shows what we trust or don't trust. Do we really believe that God is in control, and He wants what's best for us? Most of us act as if we are God, and it is our responsibility to put out every fire that comes our way. When the ledge comes calling, we need to hit our knees in prayer. Before the ledge comes calling, we should hit our knees in prayer. Maybe this situation that you are facing will be a huge dramatic monster, or maybe it won't be anything. No matter how the situation turns out, a praying Christian can find peace from Jesus. Now it's not always instant. Sometimes the ledge's voice is so loud that I have to pray even louder. Prayers aren't like vending machines where we put in something and instantly get what we want. If prayer equals Jesus guarding our hearts and minds, then that means we are in a battle. With Jesus, we can take every thought captive and not allow thoughts to take us to the ledge.

A Great Story about a Donkey

One day a farmer's donkey fell into a well. The animal cried piteously for hours as the farmer tried to figure out what to do. Finally, he decided the animal was old and the well needed to be covered up anyway; it just wasn't worth it to retrieve the donkey. He invited all his neighbors to come over and help him. They all grabbed a shovel and began to shovel dirt into the well. At first, the donkey realized what was happening and cried horribly. Then to everyone's amazement, he quieted down. A few shovel loads later, the farmer looked down the well and was astonished at what he saw. With every shovel of dirt that hit his back, the donkey was doing something amazing. He would shake it off and take a step up. As the farmer's neighbors continued to shovel dirt on top of the animal, he would shake it off and take a step up. Pretty soon, everyone was amazed as the donkey stepped up over the edge of the well and trotted off!

Sometimes, life throws dirt at you. Panic won't solve the problem. Praying, seeking God, and then acting appropriately will get you through. Stop having a victim's mentality. Take a deep breath. Calm down. Back off the ledge, and allow your adversity to be the thing that causes you to step into a plan of action. Shake the dust that's been thrown at you, and use it to motivate you to action.

This Chapter is still not about Basketball

The year after Lebron and the Heat lost in the Finals, they were there once again. This time it was different. Lebron was a machine. The Heat won in five games, and afterward the sports world debated just how great Lebron was. Some were putting him in the category of Magic Johnson, Kobe Bryant, and Michael Jordan. It's crazy how much one year and a few wins change things. If it's true with basketball, it might also be true in life. But like I said, this chapter is not about basketball.

Chapter Ten

This Should have been Chapter One

This should have been Chapter One. The human spirit is capable of some amazing things. There are people who have inspired themselves to do great things. There are self-made millionaires who don't rely on God. There are people who have lost amazing amounts of weight and have never prayed once for God's help. There are people who have invented things, created things, and changed the world without acknowledging God. I have a friend. I will call this friend, Dan. I'll call him Dan because that's his name. My friend, Dan, is not a runner. In fact, he has not run more than two miles in ten years. One day, Dan tells me that he can run three miles without training. Now being a guy who hates running but does it anyway, I knew that this was impossible. It took me a long time to get up to three miles. The next morning, I was going to start off jogging with Dan's wife, Danielle. She runs like a Kenyan. She's done multiple marathons and runs way faster than I do. We were going to start at the same time, but there was no way I was going to keep up with her. Now, right before we left, I tell Dan that he should come with us. He tells me that he doesn't have any shoes. I jokingly tell him to go barefoot. Next thing I know, Dan is outside running with us barefoot. It started as a joke, and it was really funny. The jog started on a gravel road. Dan ran on said road. We ran about half a mile and Dan was still trucking with us. We then made it to a main road and Dan was still with us. We laughed as he attempted to run on the yellow lines on the road. He said that it hurt his feet less to run on the yellow painted lines. At the mile marker, Danielle tells Dan that he's earned her respect. She tells him that he can quit now, and no one will think anything. Dan wouldn't quit. He wanted to prove a point. That day, Dan ran three miles with me, and he did it barefoot. When I told him how crazy that was, he said that when you put your mind to it you can do anything. That's the power of the human spirit. The human spirit is amazing. It should be. It was created in God's image. The problem is that so many of us rely only on the human spirit. We never tap into the Holy Spirit. If the human spirit is so amazing, imagine what can happen when we allow the Holy Spirit to take over our lives?

To find the life that Jesus talks about, we need more than the human spirit. To truly forgive, we need more than the human spirit. To find our identity in Jesus and to stop being consumed with what others think about us takes more than the human spirit. It takes relying on God's Spirit—every day.

Become Discontent with the Human Spirit

Most of us are content with what the human spirit can do. It's why we don't pray more. It's why we don't read our Bibles more. It's why we don't cry out and beg God for His presence. We need to become discontent with the human spirit and start relying on the Holy Spirit.

Skubala Happens

Paul says in his letter to the Philippians, "But whatever was to my profit I now consider loss for the sake of Christ. What is more, I consider everything a loss compared to the surpassing greatness of knowing Christ Jesus my Lord, for whose sake I have lost all things. I consider them rubbish, that I may gain Christ and be found in him, not having a righteousness of my own that comes from the law, but that which is through faith in Christ—the righteousness that comes from God and is by faith. I want to know Christ and the power of his resurrection and the fellowship of sharing in his sufferings, becoming like him in his death, and so, somehow, to attain to the resurrection from the dead." (Philippians 3:7-11).

Paul had accomplished many things based on his human spirit. In fact, if you read Philippians 3, you can see that he lists some of the amazing things that he was able to do. But, don't miss what Paul says in the verse above. He says that he considers all his accomplishments rubbish. I love that word. It's not an American word—rubbish. It's an English word. Now they say that in America, we speak English but we don't. We speak American. I tried to watch an English television show and I couldn't understand half of what they were saying. It was rubbish. I think the Bible translators were American and wanted to soften the affect of what Paul was saying so they used the cute English word rubbish. However, the word that Paul uses is actually stronger than the word, rubbish. The word in Greek is "skubala".

I don't remember a lot of Greek from my seminary days. However, I do remember the word skubala. I remember it because it's shocking that it's in the Bible. It's closer to an American cuss word. As a kid, I would have called this the "S" word. Now this chapter isn't about whether we are free to cuss or not. I don't think that this instance is enough proof for us to run outside and start cussing like a sailor. I think Paul used such strong language because he knew his audience could handle it. He also knew that they needed to see how serious he was about this. Please don't get hung up on skubala being a cuss word. That's not what this chapter is about. It's about what Paul thought about the human spirit. He thought that it was skubala. If you only rely on the human spirit, you will never truly experience Jesus. Paul believed in this so much that he considered his human spirit accomplishments skubala.

Our identity in other people or in our accomplishments is skubala compared to knowing Jesus. Finding Jesus is worth losing your identity. It's in Him that you truly find who you are. Jesus is worth seeking with all of your heart. On your greatest day, you might be able to accomplish something amazing, but it's not worth skubala compared to knowing Jesus.

The reason that this isn't a self-help book is because self-help won't lead you to know Jesus. I am in desperate need for Him. I need him for more than a ticket to Heaven. I need him to protect my mind, guard my heart, and help me to find my true self—a self that isn't swayed back and forth by people's opinions. Before you can apply anything in this book, you have to follow Jesus. It's His opinion that really matters. This is why this chapter should have been number 1. I'm assuming that most people who are reading this are Christians. Unfortunately, even well-meaning Christians can spend much of their time relying on their own skubala—human spirit.

The Human Spirit of Worry

Here's where the human spirit breaks down, worry. Relying on the human spirit works until you can't control a situation. When you can't control a situation, worry creeps in. For those of us who are addicted to worry, it leads to anxiety. Anxiety is worry on steroids. The human spirit is so powerful that it helps us through many situations. It's so strong that we rely on it over God, until a situation is out of our control. When we can't pay the bills, or we get a bad doctors report, or someone says something about us that tears our image apart, we start to worry. I once heard that worry is like a rocking chair. It gives you something to do, but it takes you nowhere.

If nobody has ever taught us how to rely on God, we do what we know. We rely on the human spirit—even when it lets us down. Let's look at something that Jesus says. Stick with me because, at first, it doesn't seem like this applies to worry. Jesus said, "Do not store up for yourselves treasures on earth, where moth and rust destroy, and where thieves break in and steal. But store up for yourselves treasures in heaven, where moth and rust do not destroy, and where thieves do not break in and steal. For where your treasure is, there your heart will be also." (Matthew 6:19-21).

Okay, so we are not to store up for ourselves treasures on earth. Now Jesus is talking about money, but it applies to anything that helps build your kingdom. Relying on the human spirit is a HUGE sign that you are building your kingdom here on earth. What are signs of building your kingdom? Well, if you lost everything would Jesus be enough? We need other people in our lives, but we don't need them more than we need Jesus. We need food to survive, but we don't need it more than we need Jesus. We need clothes because nudity just doesn't look good on most of us. We need things, but not more than we need Jesus. If we lost all of our stuff, our status, our image, our platform, what would we do?

There is nothing wrong with having stuff. The problem is that so often our stuff has us. Where is your treasure? Is it in stuff that will decay, get broken, and not truly satisfy? Or is it in Jesus? Now I ask you to stick with me because after Jesus talks about where our treasure is, he goes on to say, "Therefore I tell you, do not worry about your life, what you will eat or drink; or about your body, what you will wear. Is not life more important than food, and the body more important than clothes? Look at the birds of the air; they do not sow or reap or store away in barns, and yet your heavenly Father feeds them. Are you not much more valuable than they? Who of you by worrying can add a single hour to his life? And why do you worry about clothes? See how the lilies of the field grow. They do not labor or spin. Yet I tell you that not even Solomon in all his splendor was not dressed like one of these. If that is how God clothes the grass of the field, which is here today and tomorrow is thrown into the fire, will he not much more clothe you, O you of little faith? So do not worry, saying, 'What shall we eat?' or 'What shall we drink?' or 'What shall we wear?' For the pagans run after all these things, and your heavenly Father knows that you need them. But seek first his kingdom and his righteousness, and all these things will be given to you as well. Therefore do not worry about tomorrow, for tomorrow will worry about itself. Each day has enough trouble of its own." (Matthew 6:25-34).

I know that was a lot of Bible. I hope you didn't skim it. If you did, go back and read it. It's crucial.

Jesus talks about building our kingdom with our stuff. He then goes on to talk about worry. Why do we worry? It's because we are focused on our kingdom. We are worried about losing our stuff, even if our stuff is our name. Someone talks bad about you, and it wrecks you. Why? It's because we've built our kingdom around our name and someone is tearing our kingdom down. Our worry is a connection to our stuff!

Now what's the answer? Is it just to not worry? No! That would be relying on the human spirit. Jesus said the answer is to "Seek first his kingdom and his righteousness."

So how do you tell if you are relying on the human spirit? You don't seek God's kingdom first. You try it yourself. You try to will yourself to victory. You use your power, and then when it doesn't work, you seek God. That's not seeking God, first.

To find our identity in Jesus, it starts with relying on Him. It starts with seeking Him, first. When I go into a new situation where I know I'll be tempted to be shy, I often pray. I should pray every time, but sometimes I'm full of skubala. I pray that God will give me confidence in Him. I pray that I won't be fake or try too hard to impress people. I pray and ask God to help me be real. You see, I want to build God's kingdom. I want more of Him and less of me. When I build my kingdom, it leads me to worry. It leads me to insecurity because I don't measure up with others. It leads me to skubala. On the other hand, when I seek God's kingdom first, it leads to an abundant life.

How to Find Your Life

I don't know about you, but I want an abundant life. I want a life like Jesus promised. In order for that to happen, I have to die to myself and live for God's kingdom. I love what Jesus says about finding our life.

Then Jesus said to his disciples, "If anyone would come after me he must deny himself and take up his cross and follow me. For whoever wants to save his life will lose it, but whoever loses his life for me will find it. What good will it be for a man if he gains the whole world, yet forfeits his soul? Or what can a man give in exchange for his soul?" (Matthew 16:24-26).

You want to find your life? Jesus says that you must lose it in Him. What good will it be if we gain the whole world and yet lose our souls? What good would it be if we become famous and yet lose our soul? What good would it do if you win the lottery and yet lose your soul? What good would it be if you got a million Twitter followers and yet lose your soul? What good would it be if you accomplish all of your dreams but you lose your soul? The answer to all of those questions is skubala. Following Jesus is about denying ourselves. It's about seeking His kingdom. It's about losing our identity in order to find it in Him.

You can commit to put Jesus first, right now. You can commit to stop building your kingdom. This isn't a one-time decision. Jesus said to die daily. This means seeking God first, every day. When we do we have an abundant life! I don't know about you, but a full life in Jesus sounds a lot better than a full life of skubala.

Action Steps

Action steps for this chapter:

- Commit to put Jesus first by spending time praying and reading the Bible every day.
- Commit to put Jesus first by applying what you read in the Bible.
- Commit to put Jesus first by seeking Him before you go places that attempt to steal your identity—whether it's being around certain people, or building your kingdom by feeling the need to buy more stuff. Pray and ask God to help you seek Him first.
- Memorize Matthew 16:24-26. Put it someplace to help remind you whose Kingdom you are seeking. Write it out and place it on the dashboard of your car or on the mirror in your bedroom.

Chapter Eleven

Hurt People Hurt People

I am reminded on almost a weekly basis that there are a lot of people who are hurting. I received an ugly email not too long ago. The person who sent it apologized the next day. He apologized point 5 seconds before I hit the send button on a kick butt reply email. My email was about to destroy his email and the mean things that he had said. I felt like I had such a solid reply. It would have caused him to not only apologize, but also buy me a lifetime supply of Chipotle. Oh wait; I have twins. Change that to buy me two college educations for the twins and one Chipotle burrito for myself. Oh and add something nice for the Mrs., as well. It was that good of a reply email. I wasn't angry. I wasn't attacking. I knew that even if I was perfect, someone would crucify me. I felt like my email was kick butt because I was putting into practice what God had taught me.

I was literally reading over my reply email one last time when the person who sent the email came into my office. The first thing that he did was apologize for his email. He apologized before I had the chance to send my awesome reply email. He then told me about how he was hurting. His hurt was ugly. It was painful. It was real. He was hurting so badly that it spewed out in anger towards others. He didn't know how to handle his pain.

When this person left, I thought to myself, "Hurt people hurt people." Hurt people hurt others with their comments. When people hurt, they are not themselves. The email now made sense, and I was glad I never got to send my epic email reply.

This is just one of the many hurting people that I came in contact with that week. I have a friend who is going through an awful month. He's hurting. I've been pretty honest on my blog about the in-vitro fertilization process that my wife and I went through. It has opened doors to talk to a lot of people. We went through six years of infertility before we felt God led us to make our in-vitro decision. We are blessed with twins because of it. I know a couple who just went through the same in-vitro fertilization process as Monica and me, except that it didn't take. They had to travel for three hours for their treatments, and it didn't take. They are hurting. I know a homeless lady who in tears told me about the emotional pain she faces. She's hurting. There are a lot of hurting people. Maybe that is why there is so much ugliness in the world. Hurt people hurt people.

I don't think I would have come to this realization a few years ago. I needed to find my identity in Jesus. I needed to understand that even if I was perfect, someone would crucify me. I needed to understand that forgiven people forgive. I needed to understand that true life is found in building God's kingdom. Sometimes, I forget how broken we are. Sometimes, I forget that even Christians need a Savior.

Right now I'm not hurting. Right now my mind is at peace. It's my prayer that I can remember that people aren't perfect. Sometimes, people need me to show them grace. Sometimes, people need grace because they are really hurting.

When I Was Hurting

For six years my wife and I tried to get pregnant. Doctors told us it was impossible without some help, but they didn't know my God like I did. At year three, we were able to get pregnant on our own. This was God's miracle. It was the day of our appointment to see a specialist. Monica sensed that she should take a pregnancy test. She comes out of the bathroom and asks me, "What should I do now?" and then tells me that the test was positive. My response was, "I'll tell you what you do. You go back in there and take another test." I wanted to make sure the first test wasn't faulty. When the second test came back positive, I told Monica that I didn't trust that brand of test. We had bought so many pregnancy tests over the years that we started buying the cheap generic versions. I told Monica that I was going to the store to buy the real deal, and that while I was gone she needed to chug some water. I came back and two more tests came back positive. It was a miracle.

It was such a miracle that it didn't dawn on me that something could actually happen to the baby. At our seven-week appointment, our dreams were crushed! We were told that our baby didn't have a heartbeat. It was the worst pain that I've ever felt. God was good and held us incredibly close during that time.

Over the next three years, we prayed. We did multiple medical things to try and get pregnant. Nothing worked. Finally, we felt like God was leading us to go through The Jones Institute and do in-vitro fertilization. It wasn't an easy decision. On the one hand, I felt like I wasn't trusting God. On the other hand, I saw God's hand in this. What are the chances that we live 30 minutes from the leading facility for in-vitro fertilization? In fact, through this process we met a woman who traveled from California to the Jones Institute. That was a great reminder at how blessed we were. After a lot of prayer and time spent seeking wise counsel, we decided to go through with it.

In our first attempt, we got pregnant. We got pregnant with twins. Nine years earlier, while on a road trip, Monica and I had talked about how we both really wanted twins. We wrote out a list of names. Two of our top names were Reese and Hayden.

So we are once again pregnant and this time with twins. This pregnancy wasn't easy. I had to tell you about our first pregnancy so you could feel the emotions of our second. For the first 22 weeks of Monica's pregnancy, she had heavy bleeding. At one point, it was so bad we were convinced that we had lost the babies. The human spirit can only take so much. After multiple weeks of rushing to the hospital to see if we had lost our babies, I had a breakdown.

I was trying to be strong for my wife, so I was holding in a lot of emotions. After one doctor's report that was less than excellent, my mind filled with worry. One of my best friends sent me an email about a mistake on my blog. I normally really appreciate when people nicely tell me about my grammar mistakes. This time, I chewed his head off. I wasn't angry at him. I was hurting.

That night I went out for a jog. While jogging a song came on my i-Pod by Jon Foreman, the lead singer of Switchfoot. The lyrics said, "Why do I worry? Why do I freak out? God knows what I need. You know what I need." I lost it! To say I cried would be an understatement. Sometimes, women say they just need a good cry. I can't support that. I don't ever feel good crying. I think that's why I try not to. This cry wasn't just any cry. It was an ugly cry. I turned off my music and cried out to God. I didn't want to lose our babies. I didn't want to feel helpless while my wife hurt. I didn't want to lose my babies, but I had to trust that God knows best. After I cried out to God I started running again. I normally hate running, but that night it felt amazing. I felt like a burden lifted. I was at peace, and no longer hurting.

When I got home, I had to call my friend. I told him that it wasn't right but because I was hurting, I reacted in a way that I wouldn't normally act. Hurt people hurt people. He understood. He showed me grace. We are still great friends.

I tell you all of that just so you know that I've been there. I've hurt. Finding my identity in Jesus has helped me even through the hurt. If you are a Christian and you are hurting others with your actions, then you need to allow God to heal your hurt.

For me, I had to say out loud why I was hurting. I screamed that I didn't want God to take my babies. I left knowing that I wasn't in control. I left knowing that God is good. I can trust Him, and so can you.

Let's Pray

I do not believe in magical prayers that instantly fix things, but I also don't believe in not having any application. So in order to set up the application, I'd like to tell you a joke. "Knock knock." Come on play along. "Knock knock." You respond by saying, "Who's there?"

"Lettuce."

You respond by saying, "Lettuce Who?"

"Lettuce pray".

Get it? I want to give you a prayer to pray, but if you would rather pray something from your own words feel free. This prayer is based on the following verse from the Bible, "I lift up my eyes to the hills— Where does my help come from? My help comes from the Lord, the Maker of heaven and earth. He will not let your foot slip—he who watches over you will not slumber…" (Psalm 121:1-3a).

God, I lift my eyes to you. I am hurting! I know that my true help comes from you. You are the maker of heaven and earth. You are in control. You have my best interest in mind. Watch over me. Heal me. Hold me. Take my hurt and make it beautiful. In Jesus name, Amen.

Chapter Twelve

Confession is a Killer

One of the hardest parts about being a Christian is admitting that you are not perfect. Christians can be a ruthless bunch of judgmental poo poo heads, for lack of a better phrase. Sure Christians might admit to having faults, but I mean really talking about them.

I love the fact that I grew up in church. I love it! Just like people, no church is perfect and that includes the church where I grew up. It was a great place that helped me fall in love with Jesus, but it was also a place where people hid their sin. Nobody talked about sin openly. Men wore their best suits and women their nice dresses to church on Sundays. Everyone smiled as if to say, "We don't have problems." The only times that I ever remember people talking about sin was when someone got caught in it. Every once in a while a prominent member or staff member would get caught in sin. When that happened, people talked about sin a lot. Gossip flowed through the church like a tidal wave. No one ever taught me this in a sermon or lesson, but I learned quickly that if I didn't want to be embarrassed, I couldn't talk about my sin. So, I learned to play the church game. I smiled a lot. I wore my nice clothes. I talked about sin like it was something other people dealt with. The problem was and still is to this day, I'm not perfect. You don't believe me?

I'm fat. I'm too fat to look good at the beach, but not fat enough to blend in at a buffet. I like going to a buffet because it's one of the places where I can feel thin around other people. Okay that sentence alone proves I'm not perfect. That was mean. The point is, I struggle with over-eating. For me, it's not a problem of exercising. I exercise more than the average fat guy. I run three to four times a week. I've run a half marathon. I lift weights on a somewhat regular basis. I work out. I can't control myself around food. When I hear others talk about their addictions, it's like I'm listening to my own story. I go to a party, and I have a plan. My plan is to only get one plate of food. Then something happens. I end up talking to people around the food, and I gorge myself. I often leave a party feeling so guilty. Why did I do that again? I wake up the next morning, and my behavior haunts me. I vow to do better the next time, but I rarely do. I'm not perfect.

Besides having a food addiction, I get really ticked off at other drivers. When someone cuts me off, I don't honk. I don't give them the bird. I call them, out loud, a "jack hole." What's a jack hole? Well, it's the first part of a certain cuss word, minus the cuss word combined with the second part of a different cuss word minus the cuss word. It's my way of getting around cussing. It's wrong. The intention is the same as cussing. I'm angry. I didn't get my way. I'm impatient. I throw that word around in the privacy of my car, but God sees my actions. I'm not perfect.

Another weakness of mine: It's not easy for me to guard my eyes. Let me be specific. I can't have Netflix streaming because it has movies that contain nudity. I can't go to the theater if a movie has nudity because it's too big of a temptation. I can't have HBO, Showtime, or Skinamax… I mean Cinemax on my TV. I have to work hard at bouncing my eyes. What's bouncing your eyes? It's when you see an attractive girl and everything in you wants to stare at her like she was a piece of meat, but instead you bounce your eyes. You turn your eyes the other direction. If I allowed myself, I could be consumed with lust. I love my wife, but even more, I love God. Before I even met my wife, God convicted me about the things I was putting before my eyes. I would rent movies that I knew had brief nudity in them. Most everyone had seen them, and it wasn't like it was full blown porn. One time when I was about to watch something, I heard a still small voice say, "What would your students think if they saw you watching this?" From that day on, I started bouncing my eyes. I would look the other way when I wanted to stare. I stopped renting movies that fed my evil desire. I've seen way too many Godly men ruin their families and their ministries because of an addiction to lust. On a side note, I've also seen a lot of guys freed from this addiction. For me, it took investing in a better story. My story was helping a group of students fall in love with Jesus. That was enough to get me to stop feeding my fleshly desire to lust. For others though it takes more than that. I have a friend who sought professional Christian counseling. My friend found freedom in a support group called Celebrate Recovery. If you are a guy, you are most likely tempted with lust. You can find freedom, but you have to be willing to flee. Even now I have to constantly flee. If I let down my guard or allow even a little taste of lust into my life, I will dive in full force.

See what I mean? I'm not perfect. Now I talked about some of the things I struggle with, but there are more. I'm in desperate need of Jesus and others to keep me accountable.

What AA and Weight Watchers Know

Too many Christians play the perfect game. They act like sin only happens to the other guy. Let me ask you a question. Who knows about your sin? Is it just you and God? How's that going for you? Are you overcoming it?

I mentioned this in an earlier chapter, but AA and Weight Watchers have something that most Christians are sorely lacking—a confession group. We need someone to check in with. We need someone to check in with us.

The Healing Power Of Confession

"Therefore confess your sins to each other and pray for each other so that you may be healed. The prayer of a righteous man is powerful and effective" (James 5:16).

Confession is not only good for the soul, it's good for our entire being. James says that we will be healed when we confess. I don't know if he's talking about physical or spiritual healing. Either way, it sounds good to me. Maybe he's even talking about both. You sin. I sin. We all sin. We aren't perfect. We know that, yet we still try to hide behind the mask of perfection. We pretend to be better than we really are. You want to know what would happen if Christians started confessing their sins before one another? Revival. How do I know? I've seen it. When I was in high school, a group from a Christian college came to share their story. They had experienced an amazing spiritual revival at their school. It started when one student stood up and confessed a sin before the entire school body. That one confession led to months of spiritual revival. It was so powerful, churches wanted to experience it. In fact, my church brought in some of the students, and guess what happened? Revival. People started confessing their sins. Meetings were supposed to be a couple of nights for one week, and ended up lasting for multiple weeks. This same church that didn't normally talk about sin was now confessing sins during the service. Night after night, people talked about their struggles. It was more powerful than any sermon I'd ever heard. Then it stopped. What was so great for a few weeks stopped. People went back to their old facades.

Your sin is ugly. My sin is ugly. The thought of standing up before your church to talk about your sin is probably petrifying. So let's lower the scale. What would it take for you to talk about your sin to one person? Who is one person that you know that wouldn't judge you for confessing your sin? If you can't think of anyone, then get down on your knees and beg God to bring someone into your life. We need to find freedom. You need to find freedom.

Sin Finds Us Out

Most people don't have anyone to confess to. So instead of finding freedom, they hide. Eventually sin has a way of exposing itself. We think we can keep it hidden, but eventually it comes out. Either we don't know of another way to get out of our sin, so we in essence want to get caught, or we slip up so badly, we can't hide it anymore. Sin will find us out.

What are you feeling right now? Are you feeling like this is asking too much? Are you rationalizing your sin by saying that it's really not a big deal? If you break down the word rationalize it's rational lies. I kid...but not really. When we rationalize our sin we are lying to ourselves. Are you allowing fear to keep you in hiding? Is Jesus your identity? For a lot of Christians, our identity becomes the game we play at church. We become Baptist Bob or Deacon Dale. We become Susie Sunday school teacher or Pete the pastor. If you go to church long enough, you will get elevated to some responsibility. There are never enough people to do all of the work, so I promise you it will eventually happen. You will get a little responsibility, and then you will think to yourself, "I've got to play the game." What would the people who look up to you think of you if they found out about your secret sin? You know what they'd think because you've seen them judge others. So instead of finding freedom, you live with your secret sin. Not anymore. It's time to confess. It's time to find freedom. It's time! Jesus is your identity and that means that you are forgiven. God sees you as He sees His son. The problem with confession for most of us is not that we don't trust God's forgiveness; it's that we do not trust other people. Here's what you might find if you confessed your sin to another solid, Bible believing, Christian. You might find that the person will still love you. In fact, it might even spur this person on to share his/ her sin. Now if the person judges you or condemns you, shake the dust and move on. Here's what I've found. Even as a pastor (when I get the guts to confess my sin to other believers) they often respect me even more than when they thought I was perfect. I've shared some of my hidden sins with some guys in my church. They still listen to me preach. They are still my friends. They still respect me. Ten years ago, I couldn't confess to anyone because I had to pretend to be perfect. Today, I'm an open book. I still revert to old habits from time to time. I still try to hide things, but thankfully, I have friends who pry into my life. I'm not perfect, so I've stopped pretending to be. You are not perfect, so it's time to stop pretending to be. Confess your sin, first to God, and then to someone else. The accountability of relationship will help you overcome the secret sin battle. Do you like your sin more than you like the idea of freedom? If that's the case, then you still haven't found your identity in Jesus.

As a Christian, Jesus has forgiven you for your sin: Your past sin. Your current sin. Your future sin. At the same time, there is a Biblical mandate to confess our sins one to another. Our sin is gross like skubala. When we don't confess, we carry with us extra weight. Confession lightens the load. It doesn't change God's perspective of you. He loves you period. Confession changes your perspective of God. It's a daily reminder that He's cleaned up your mess. I think the Catholics have it right in that they practice confession. I think they have it wrong in that they go to a priest. We have a high priest named Jesus that we can confess to. We also should confess to those who we've hurt and those who can keep us accountable.

Apply This Thing

Here's the application for this chapter. Find one person you can trust, and confess your sin. I recommend someone other than your spouse. Find a fellow Christian of the same sex and ask if he/she can handle your confession about your sin. Then be open and honest about it. Start off by taking a baby step. Tell someone your smallest struggle, or the thing you are least embarrassed about. See how the person handles that, and then move to the next thing. Develop such a strong relationship that you know you can confess anything, and this person will not judge you. It takes time. Start small, but start somewhere.

Chapter Thirteen

Let's Not Give Them Something to Talk About

"Live your life in such a way that if anyone should speak badly of you, no one will believe it" (Plato, paraphrase). Christians are called to a higher standard. We aren't perfect—far from it. However, we are forgiven and are challenged to live differently. Regardless of how great of a person you are, someone will talk smack about you.

I was doing some research for a sermon, and I was trying to find a quote from Billy Graham. I went to Google and found more than I wanted. Apparently, not everyone loves Billy Graham. He is known for his legendary integrity. He was never involved in a sexual scandal. He shined bright through the 80's when other TV evangelists became gossip magazine ammunition. According to some sources, Billy Graham isn't even a Christian. I read some of the blog hate thrown at him, and I was blown away. Billy Graham is possibly the greatest evangelist to ever live.

He's up there with the great men and women of the Bible. He's what MC Hammer would call "2 Legit 2 Quit." He's done amazing things for God, yet some have found a way to criticize him. Billy Graham is an amazing man of God. He's lived such an amazing life that even when people bash on him, it holds no ground. In fact, he's lived such an amazing life that the bloggers who were throwing hate his way, just looked silly.

Now I'm no Billy Graham. At the same time, I hope to live my life in such a way that even when the haters hate, the people who know me best won't believe it.

Peter vs. Judas

One of Jesus' closest friends was definitely not perfect. Peter was his name and he's known for his "gigantor" foot in his mouth type blunders. Peter is the guy who denied knowing Jesus. He's also the guy Jesus called "Satan." Peter, however, is wicked awesome because he learned from his blunders. Ever wonder what separates Peter from another one of Jesus' follower's, Judas? Judas betrayed Jesus and then took his life. Peter denied he knew Jesus, but ends up leading the church. Both men made HUGE mistakes, but we still name our kids after Peter. There aren't any little kids named Judas running around the playgrounds. Peter was able to move on from his big mistakes. He was able to live such an amazing life that his letters were included in the Bible. Peter wasn't bound by his mistakes. He learned from them. So when Peter wrote the following, I think he knew what he was talking about.

"Dear friends, I urge you, as aliens and strangers in the world, to abstain from sinful desires, which war against your soul. Live such good lives among the pagans that, though they accuse you of doing wrong, they may see your good deeds and glorify God on the day he visits us" (1 Peter 2:11-12).

You are not perfect. Some people will hold your imperfections against you. Some people will accuse you of doing wrong, even when you didn't. You can't please all people, all the time. You can only please God. When we live for Jesus, it fuels us to live a good life. When we live for Jesus, it ultimately leads people to glorify God. That's HUGE! Why should we abstain for the sinful desires that war against our souls? Peter says that it's because our lives should lead pagans to glorify our God. Even when others accuse us of doing wrong, they should see our Jesus in the way that we respond to them.

Haters are going to Hate

Haters are going to hate, but don't let that distract you from following Jesus. Think about it…people have said all sorts of hateful and mean things towards Jesus, even to this day. People misquote Him, hate on His church, and misrepresent Him. I mean, every second of every day someone is saying something wrong about Jesus. However, people still accept Jesus every Sunday in churches around the world; people also accept Jesus every day in personal encounters with other Christians. That's amazing! When your identity is in Jesus, it leads you to want to live for Him—not to make a great name for yourself, but to bring glory to Jesus. Haters are going to hate, and there is nothing you can do about it. You can try to respond to all the haters, but it won't help. You can worry about what they say, but it won't get you anywhere. All you can do is pray, and move on. Live such an amazing life for Jesus that even when people hate on you, those who know you best, won't believe it for a second. Let your life speak for itself. When you live to honor God, you don't have to fight back at critics because your integrity and character will have already fought the fight for you.

A few years ago I told a story on my blog in an attempt to be funny. My wife and I went on vacation with our friend Jamey. Jamey loves the Waffle House. He calls it "One of those fancy restaurants where they cook in front of you." Well, on our way home Jamey requested we go to Waffle House for dinner. We were somewhere in North Carolina and the accent of our waitress was so thick we couldn't understand her when she told us what city we were in. The place was crawling with hunters that had an ever-glowing neck the color of bright red. As we were leaving, Monica and Jamey went to the restrooms. There I was standing by myself in a room full of men who support the right to bear arms. I saw the jukebox and I proceeded to play three songs. The first song was, "There's A Special Lady Waiting for Me at the Waffle House." Yes it's a real song. The second song was a country classic. The third song was…wait for it…wait for it…Clay Aiken's "Measure Of A Man." Now if that song was played anywhere else it wouldn't' have been funny to me, but in that Waffle House I found it to be really funny. When Monica and Jamey came out of the restroom I said, "We've got to get out of here now!" I quickly ushered them out of there like I stole something. When we got in the car I told them what I did and they laughed.

I put that story on my blog and it never dawned on me that I was going to upset Claymates. What's a Claymate? It's the passionate fans of the second season of American Idol's Clay Aiken. They came out in force against my post. They said that if that's the type of hate that I was going to spew they would never visit my church. I honestly didn't' mean anything against Clay. If anything it was more about the Waffle House. I was wrestling with whether or not I should respond to the attacks when my faithful blog readers started coming to my defense. They didn't' attack back. They simply let them know who I was and that I didn't mean any harm by the post. I love that I was so consistent with loving Jesus and loving others that I didn't have to defend myself. Other people knew my heart. Haters are going to hate, but we can live such a good life that their hate won't stick to us.

Application

Who are you plugged into? Who is your community? Who do you invest in so much that even when people spew hate it won't stick? The key is not just to be known to be known. You need to invest in a group of people. People that you can show the love of God to. If you don't have a group then you need to find one. Whether it's by finding a church or joining a small group at the church that you attend. You also need to get out and live such a good life among the lost that they glorify God by watching you live.

Chapter Fourteen

The Shortest Chapter in this Book

The Bible says, "Do not pay attention to every word people say, or you may hear your servants cursing you—for you know in your heart that many times you yourself have cursed others" (Ecclesiastes 7:21-22).

Put that in your pipe and...well...hold on to it. Unless you are one of the deacons at some of the Baptist churches where I've worked, you might not be able to relate to sucking on nicotine sticks. How about this...put that in your mouth and eat it. If there is one thing that good Christians know how to do, it's eat. Seriously though, think about that verse. You are not perfect and neither is anyone else. There are some words that people say that we just need to ignore. Truth be told, we also have talked smack about many people. Part of learning your identity is allowing God's words to hold more power over you than man's words. People talk skubala about other people. We shouldn't do it, but it happens. Let's not pay such close attention to every word people say about us, and acknowledge that there have been times when we have talked skubala about others.

Chapter Fifteen

A Test

I love my wife! I often talk about her on my blog. For a recent birthday, I posted the following on my blog:

Today my wife turns extra beautiful. It's her birthday. Now I hear it's not nice to share a woman's age, so I'm going to randomly pull out a number and say that number of nice things about my wife. Here are 32 things that amaze me about my wife...

1. She watches *The Walking Dead* with me. This isn't a girly show, yet it's a show that we both really enjoy watching together.
2. She finds me attractive. I'm balding, overweight, and I have hair on my back. My wife, for some reason, finds me incredibly attractive.
3. She doesn't nag me. Nagging wives are such a...well...nag.
4. She's a great mom! I love how much our kids love her.

5. She's incredibly patient with me. I don't always take initiative. I often forget to do things. I'm not a perfect spouse, yet she has never put me down or made me feel like an idiot.

6. She loves what I love. She took me to my first Laker game. She watches the playoffs with me. She even watches *SportsCenter* when I'm out of town and then fills me in when I get back.

7. She loves Jesus. The Bible says, "Charm is deceptive, and beauty is fleeting; but a woman who fears the LORD is to be praised." Here's what that means. External beauty is fleeting. Eventually all people kind of end up looking the same, old and wrinkly. There are no attractive people in the old folks' home. I'm thankful that I'm married to someone who is beautiful on the outside and the inside. You want to know what separates truly beautiful women? They love Jesus.

8. She's funny. My wife makes me laugh. It's not easy to make me laugh but she does.

9. She reads my blog and proofs it daily. I make a lot of stupid mistakes. I often mix up then and than. I often put your when it should be you're. She reads my blog first thing in the morning and then lets me know, in a loving way, what mistakes I've made.

10. She likes Vampire movies and TV shows but doesn't force me to watch them.

11. She likes to be silly with me. I'm pretty goofy. She does more than tolerate it. She joins the fun.

12. She once drove one hour to buy me Chipotle. Before we had our very own Chipotle in the 757, we had to drive an hour for it. One day during the summer, I came home and had Chipotle waiting for me. Just because.

13. She doesn't ask me to buy her girly products at the store. Girl stuff freaks me out. She knows it. She respects my freaking and doesn't ask me to buy it for her.

14. She can name the entire starting five and most of the bench players for the Lakers. She learned this without me asking her to. She did it because they are my favorite team.

15. She doesn't go to the bathroom in front of me. I know this is weird, but I think that it ruins the romance. Ten years of marriage and she still allows me to be weird like that.

16. She invests in people. My wife has invited more people to our church than anyone I know. There are lots of families who are now a part of church because of my wife's investment.

17. She believes in me.

18. She is confident in who she is.

19. She helps me pick out my clothes. Before I got married, I would look at what the mannequins in the store were wearing and then buy it. Not anymore.

20. She buys me a Full Throttle Energy drink before I preach.

21. She's pretty.

22. She's so thoughtful. She is always thinking about nice things that we can do to be a blessing to others.

23. She loves road trips. We love to travel together.

24. She stokes the fire of our marriage. Fires start off big but over time they dwindle. It's the same thing with marriage. Often marriages start off blazing, but the fire quickly dwindles. Ten years into our marriage, and we are still in love.

25. She bought me the complete Rocky collection even though she hates Rocky. I love Rocky.

26. She's a great cook! She looks for new recipes and makes food that is loaded with yummy goodness.

27. She's okay with us not owning a pet. She grew up with a dog and a cat. I think owning a pet is like using your cash money as toilet paper. It just doesn't make sense to me.

28. She gently reminds me where the turns are. I stink at directions. She could make fun of me, but she doesn't. She gently tells me where to turn.

29. She gently rolls me over when I'm snoring. Half the time I don't even remember her waking me up. That's love.

30. She is one of the most selfless people that I know. She inspires me.

31. She's not dramatic. I think I wouldn't last long if I was with someone who was high drama.

32. She's the best thing to ever happen to me. God knew what He was doing when he blessed me with Monica. My life is full because of her.

Monica, happy birthday. I love you more.

Now one of the things that I love about having a blog is the comments that people leave. The vast majority of comments are filled with awesome. I do however get the occasional negative comment. There was one comment that really tested my ability to put into practice what God has taught me. It came on the blog post about my wife for her birthday. It inspired me to write a post to the author who went by the name Blown Away.

Dear Blown Away,

This week you left a comment on my blog, and I wanted to say thank you. Just in case you forgot, let me post it below…

I hardly ever read your blog anymore because I find it quite disturbing, so I really don't know what made me read it today. I was with you until #30. Seriously? From what I see you are 2 of the most selfish people I've ever come across in my life! The fact that you consider yourselves and each other to be selfless just blows me away because I know neither of you are stupid or uneducated! I really just thought you chose to be so selfish and were doing it on purpose because it's so blatant and obvious, but when you publicly proclaim each other as selfless on your blog for the world to see, I don't quite know how to take that. I guess it just makes me feel sorry for you that you can't see it and you don't have anyone in your lives who love you enough to tell you that you come across that way so you can correct it.

Like I said, I want to thank you. Now, don't get me wrong. What you said was evil and mean and straight from the pits of Hell. I'm not thanking you because what you did was right. I'm thanking you because you tested me.

Three years ago, I couldn't have handled your comment. I'm a certified people-pleaser. Three years ago, your comment would have consumed me. What happened three years ago changed me?

I heard God whisper, "Even if you were perfect, somebody would crucify you." That phrase is something that I believe. It's something that I preach. I'm not defined by people's opinions. I'm defined by Jesus. He loves me despite my selfishness and patiently works to make me better.

After reading your comment, some people told me that I should punch you in the throat. Other people told me that I should be angry. I mean, after all, you tried to sabotage a post celebrating my wife, and you attacked both of us. I don't know if you care or not, but I'm not angry at you. In fact, I'd like to hug you. I feel like you might need a hug. Or maybe a tickle fight? I'm kidding about the tickle fight. It's a little joke I have. It's funny to think about two adults having a tickle fight.

I smiled after I read your comment because it didn't bother me. I'm not perfect, but I've come a long way with my people pleasing disease.

I know you will probably never admit to writing the comment. You wrote it anonymously, and the email address that you registered doesn't work. I tried to email you at 1234@aol.com. I thought it was a bogus email by the fact that it said aol. Who uses that anymore? The only thing that would have given it away more is if it was from Juno. Are you still on MySpace? I digress…

Anyway, I just want to say that if you do visit my blog again on this day, please know that I'm praying for you. I prayed for you multiple times throughout the day. I'm not praying that you will learn to like me. I'm praying that you will forgive me if I've wronged you, and that you will become an encourager instead of a discourager. Even if you never change, I still thank you. Thank you for showing me that I'm not as consumed with people's opinions as I once was.

Thanks again,
robshep.com

I am pleased at where God has brought me. That post would have destroyed my day before I came to know who I am in Jesus. In fact, I probably would have spent the entire week trying to figure out who sent it. Now, it doesn't matter. I was tested, and I passed. I hope that through my story, you will be inspired to fall in love with Jesus and know that you are His. My prayer is that if you are ever tested, you, too, will pass. You can pass because you know that, "Even if you were perfect, somebody would crucify you".

Chapter Sixteen

The Freedom to Say "No"

One HUGE sign of being a people pleaser is the fear of saying, "No." We are so afraid of letting someone down that we over commit. Those of us who are "over-committers" often burn ourselves out because we are constantly saying, "Yes."

There is a another group that struggles with saying "No," and they aren't over-committers. They are the ones who say, "Yes," and then never show up. I often wonder if these people just hope that others forget that they committed to attend. I see this all the time with weddings. If you RSVP for a wedding, it means that you have known about that wedding for a while. It also means that someone has paid for a meal for you to eat. To just not show up is really selfish. But, I get it. You get the invitation, and you don't want to let that person down. You say, "Yes." Then the day of the wedding comes, and you are tired because you never say, "No." "The thought of taking the time to put on your monkey suit or nice dress wears you out. You start to excuse it. You think, "Maybe they won't notice that I'm not there." You invent a legit excuse. "I have a really bad headache." Followed by a muffled, under the breath, "after hitting my head against a concrete wall over and over again, so I don't have to come to your wedding."

You may be afraid to say, "No," and you over- commit, or you are afraid to say, "No," but don't show. Both are signs that your identity is in other people's opinions of you.

Let Your Yes Be Yes

"Simply let your 'Yes' be 'Yes,' and your 'No,' 'No'; anything beyond this comes from the evil one." ~ Jesus (Matthew 5:37).

I don't know if I fully understand Jesus' statement. I know it's important because he said it. I know it's extra important because his brother James also says it in his letter in the Bible. It's the last part that I am still wrapping my brain around. The part that says, "... anything else comes from the evil one." So my "Maybe" comes from Satan? In context, Jesus was saying this about making oaths to God. In His time, people would swear by things. It is almost like, in our time, when someone prays "God, if you get me out of this mess, I promise I will never drink alcohol again." The promise becomes too big and eventually you break it. The problem is that you've broken your promise to God, and that's a big deal.

Jesus wants us to stick to our word. Let yes be yes, and let no be no. So Jesus doesn't want us to make a bunch of empty promises that we won't keep. He wants our heart—our commitment to yes, or no.

So Jesus' brother, James, comes along and says essentially the same thing. The people in his time were swearing by God's name that what they were saying was true. We still do this today. You tell someone an unbelievable true story, and they respond by saying, "That didn't happen". In that moment, your response might just be,

"I swear to God." It's as if swearing to God or on our mother's grave will give credence to the story. James comes along and says simply, "Let your yes be yes and your no be no." In other words, speak the truth and don't worry about convincing others of it. You don't need to swear by God to make your point. If someone doesn't believe you, it's okay. You've told the truth. God knows your heart. That person is not your judge.

Whew…Freedom

Now, what does all this have to do with us being able to say yes or no to people when they ask us to do something? Great question. As Christians we represent Jesus. We are the hands and feet of God on this earth. In fact, we are the only Jesus that some people know. So when someone asks you to do something, and you can't tell them "No" because of your fear of hurting them, you are misrepresenting Jesus. When you over commit and end up showing up at events burnt out and tired, you misrepresent Jesus. When you say "Yes" to something and then you don't show up, you misrepresent Jesus. On the other hand, when we find our identity in Jesus, we don't have to bear the weight of other's opinions. If someone asks us to do something we can say, "Let me check my schedule." That always buys me some time to gather my thoughts and think through whether or not I should commit to the request. After some time of thinking and praying, I can then give a firm yes or no. When I say, "No," I don't have to feel the pressure to explain it away. I can simply say, "I'm sorry, but I'm not able to go." Explaining it away makes us look like we are coming up with excuses. I know it's our attempt to be nice, but in reality it's our attempt to make sure others don't judge us. We get to say "No" but still feel good about ourselves because our excuse is so great there is no way others can get angry at us. Stop it! Simply let your yes be yes and your no be no. Say, "No" to people. Say, "No" often—not in a mean way or as a jerk but as a person who understands that it is not possible to be all things to all people.

The Value of Your Yes

"Whatever you say yes to in life means less for something already there. Make sure the yes is worth the less." ~ Louie Giglio.

I love that quote by pastor, author, and godfather of the modern worship movement, Louie Giglio. When you say yes to something it means that you are saying no to something else. Your yes to a party may mean saying no to spending alone time with your spouse or kids. Saying yes to a great opportunity means saying no to some of the opportunities you currently have. We each have only twenty-four hours in a day. We can't invent more time. If I say yes to working out early in the morning, it means I'm saying no to sleep. If you say yes for your children to join a select sports team that plays on Sundays, it means that you are saying no to church attendance. What type of message does that send to your kids? What type of message does it send to God? What if we said, "Yes" to God and trusted that He would provide a better opportunity than the one we said "No" to? The point is that when we say, yes or no, it has incredible power. Learning whose we are gives us the freedom to say yes or no because ultimately we are saying yes or no to what is most important.

If we say, "No" and someone doesn't understand then big whoop dee do. Well, I know it's a big whoop dee do because I struggle with this, but stick with me. At the end of the day, God's opinion matters the most. We first need to prioritize our yes around things that honor God. If you are not a morning person, then prioritize your yes around your night time schedule. Say, "No" to watching TV until you are tired and say, "Yes" to spending time with God. Say, "Yes" to God first, and "No" to things that get in the way of having a dynamic relationship with Him.

Next, prioritize your yes around your family. You may love to play in that bowling league or adult softball league or in that online video game, but if saying, "Yes" to that means saying, "No" to your family then your priorities are skewed. I think one area where people miss this greatly is with where they live. People pick a place to live based off of a job. That's not bad but it's often times saying no to other great things. If you say yes to a job that moves you far away from family and friends then you are saying no to community. Sure you can find a new community, but it's not always easy. Now if God calls you to move away then of course you move. The point though is that many people say yes because of a job advancement, and they don't think through what they are saying no to.

Finally, prioritize your yes around friends and other people. You need other people, so make time for them. However, you don't need all people. You may have to say, "No" to something good because you've already committed your "Yes" to something better.

I got invited to an amazing conference in California. It was a great chance for me to connect with some great people, hear some amazing speakers, and meet some of my preaching heroes. I went the year before, and it was a highlight of my year. In fact, I heard a message at that conference that challenged me to make a HUGE change in my life. I had to pay for my flight, but my hotel, conference, and food were paid. When talking to my wife, she expressed how stressed she had been juggling the end of a school year (she was a teacher), our twins, and the start of our new church plant. Even though she was stressed, she gave her approval for me to go to this conference. Even though it was a great opportunity, I decided it wasn't worth it. Because I ended up saying, "No" to the conference, I was able to say, "Yes" to my wife. She was able to get some much needed down time with friends, and I was given the opportunity to hang out with my then one year old twins. While I was having a daddy day teaching my kids how to make fart noises, going to Toys R Us, eating the samples at Costco, and chasing them around the house, I didn't think once about the conference. I said, "No" to something good that allowed me to say, "Yes" to something better.

I'm Not the Authority on This

One of the hardest things about writing a book or preaching a sermon is the sense of authority that comes from the author or speaker. I am not the authority on this! I struggle greatly with saying, "No." I fear that people will judge me or think badly about me. I fear that I can't be all things to all people. I fear that I will miss out, so I burn myself out by saying, "Yes." to way too much. I am learning and then re-learning how to let my yes be yes and my no be no. I'm learning how to say, "No" to great opportunities, so that I can say, "Yes" to God opportunities. I'm learning to overcome my fear of saying, "No."

Chapter Seventeen

Fear Not !

I once heard that the command that is given the most in the Bible is "Fear not." Until I heard a speaker say this, I had never noticed how often this command is given. It's said a lot. In fact, almost every book in the Bible has a verse that says, "Fear not." Well, that is if you read the King James Bible. If you read the KJV, you will also see words like "hither," "thou," and they call donkeys curse words. You've been warned. I digress.

Even if you don't read the Bible in the King James Version, you will see the phrase, "Do not fear." So if it's in the Bible so much, the appropriate question that we should be asking is why? Why does God not want us to fear?

Fear God

Before we answer the "Fear not" question, we must talk about what God wants us to fear. God wants us to fear Him. Don't believe me?

- Leviticus 25:17 "Do not take advantage of each other, but fear your God. I am the Lord your God."
- Deuteronomy 5:29 "Oh, that their hearts would be inclined to fear me and keep all my commands always, so that it might go well with them and their children forever!"
- Deuteronomy 6:24 "The Lord commanded us to obey all these decrees and to fear the Lord our God, so that we might always prosper and be kept alive, as is the case today."
- Joshua 24:14 "Now fear the Lord and serve him with all faithfulness. Throw away the gods your forefathers worshiped beyond the River and in Egypt, and serve the Lord."
- 1 Samuel 12:24 "But be sure to fear the Lord and serve him faithfully with all your heart; consider what great things he has done for you."
- Psalm 19:9 "The fear of the Lord is pure, enduring forever. The ordinances of the Lord are sure and altogether righteous."
- Proverbs 1:7 "The fear of the Lord is the beginning of knowledge, but fools despise wisdom and discipline."
- Ecclesiastes 12:13 "Now all has been heard; here is the conclusion of the matter: Fear God and keep his commandments, for this is the whole duty of man."
- Luke 1:50 "His mercy extends to those who fear him, from generation to generation."
- Luke 12:4-5 "I tell you, my friends, do not be afraid of those who kill the body and after that can do no more. But I will show you whom you should fear: Fear him who, after the killing of the body, has power to throw you into hell. Yes, I tell you, fear him."

I told you. Now, before you translate those verses to God saying, "boo" and run off scared like one of those girls in a horror movie, let's make a distinction between a holy fear and a horror fear. Currently, in the world in which I live, I don't see a lot of holy fear. There isn't a lot of sacredness or reverence. There is more of a mindset of whatever feels good do it. A holy fear is a deep respect. It's kind of like this. In school, I rarely respected a substitute teacher. A substitute was basically there so that we could goof off. Nobody paid attention. In fact, I remember one time a friend of mine, Michael Jackson, danced all the way to the front of the classroom and back as the sub stood there frozen. The best part was when he spun and yelled "Whoo hoo" in a high pitched Michael Jackson voice. There was no fear or respect for the substitute teacher. Now contrast that with Mr. Bolden. Mr. Bolden carried a BIG stick when he taught. He would often slam it down on a desk, just for effect. Now before you picture him being a huge brute, you need to know he was tall and skinny. He was ha-larious. He made history so much fun. In fact, when we were learning about the Civil War, he did a fake amputation in the classroom. It was intense. It wasn't real, but he used a real person and some Hollywood magic. He showed us movie clips of the wars we were studying. He was my favorite teacher. He was fun, yet students never crossed him. His tests were difficult. The same students who would abuse a substitute, never acted up for Mr. Bolden. Why? We had a high level of respect. We had a holy fear. We didn't want to cross him, but at the same time, we loved spending time with him. Maybe that's what God is looking for when He desires that we fear Him?

We should have such awe for God that it leads to obedience. We should have such a respect for God that we choose Him over everything else. We should fear God because He has our life in His hands, but at the same time we should not be afraid of His hands. Pastor and author John Piper says, "The fear of the Lord is so awesome that you would not dare run away from Him but that you would dare to run to him." I love that!

We should trust that God is good. However, just because God is good, doesn't mean that we should walk all over Him, like my class used to walk all over a substitute. God is good, but He is just. The Bible is clear that God disciplines those He loves. Now we don't have to be afraid that God is going to get us every time we make a mistake. God is not the bully who plucks the wings off of a fly and then burns said fly with a magnifying glass. God is a perfect example of a father. He loves us, unconditionally. When He disciplines us, it's for our own good. It's to help us become more like Him.

Back to the Fear Not Question

Now because we should fear God, we can understand the "Fear not" question. Ultimately we should fear not because we can trust that God is good. Abraham had every reason to be afraid. God promises him a son and then requests that he sacrifice his son on an altar. Abraham trusted that God was good, and in the end God provided for Abraham. Mary, Jesus' mother, had every reason to be afraid. As a virgin in her culture, she could be stoned for getting pregnant out of wedlock. She also should be afraid because it was difficult for a woman to provide a living for herself in that culture. Without a husband, there would be no way for her to provide for her baby. Yet the message that the angel of the Lord declared to Mary was, "Fear not." Why? We are on God's side. We can trust that God has a plan and that His plans are wicked awesome! Daniel had every right to be afraid. He was thrown in a lions' den to be the main course. Only the next morning, observers came to find out that Daniel had been having tickle fights all night long with the lions. Okay, he didn't have tickle fights, but I'm not sure what else he did. Daniel had every reason to fear man. Yet, even when it was the darkest time in his life, he trusted that God is good. Shadrach, Meshach, and Abednego refused to be afraid of what the king could do to them. The king made a decree that whoever wouldn't bow down to his statue would be killed. Shadrach, Meshach, and Abednego wouldn't bow down because they feared God more than they feared man. Those jokers got thrown into the fire, only to see God come through for them. They were spared, and the king was shown just how powerful God is. Even in those times when God doesn't come through like we want Him to, we should trust that God is good. Our fear of God should lead us not to fear even the worst circumstances.

Fear is a Great Motivator but an Awful Master

I once watched a documentary on Type 2 diabetes. It freaked this fat boy out. I immediately went on a diet, started jogging, and lost 15 pounds. Oh, and I started taking cinnamon pills. Apparently raw cinnamon helps prevent diabetes. Fear motivated me to action, but it didn't master me. It didn't keep me up at night. It didn't cause me to worry about things that hadn't come true yet. It motivated me to action. We should have a healthy fear of things. People with pet snakes scare me. We should have a healthy fear of snakes! We should have a healthy fear of driving in the car without a seatbelt. We should fear walking down dark alleys by ourselves in the middle of the night. There are some things that we should cause a healthy fear.

Most of us, though, allow fear to be our master. We become afraid of the "what if." What if this person doesn't like me, what if I try and then fail, what if, etc. When fear is your master, it freezes you from doing what God has called you to do.

The late novelist John Gardner said, "One of the reasons why mature people stop growing and learning is that they become less and less willing to risk failure." I think this is why the saying, "You can't teach an old dog new tricks" has been around so long. I don't know about you, but I don't want to be an old dog! In fact, I want to be like

Colonel Sanders. Sanders had many jobs, including: steamboat pilot, insurance salesman, railroad fireman, and farmer. After Sander's wife left him and took his kids, her brother wrote him the following letter; "She had no business marrying a no-good fellow like you who can't hold a job." Colonel Sanders failed at everything in his life until he was 70. Around the age of 70, he started doing what he always wanted to do in the first place and that was cook chicken. At the age of 70 Colonel Sanders started franchising Kentucky Fried Chicken, and it's now one of the largest fast food chains in the world. How awesome is that?

When we learn to fear God, people become a lot less scary. Most of the time we don't attempt to do great things for God because we are afraid. I wonder how many of those reading this are making fear decisions and not faith decisions. Faith is the evidence of things unseen. It is trusting in a God that we can't see to do what we cannot see yet. It's taking such a big leap that it forces you to rely on God. It's the type of faith that draws you to your knees. Most of us will never experience that type of faith because we are paralyzed by fear.

I love what author and pastor Mark Batterson says. "We need to stop living as if the purpose of life is to arrive safely at death. Instead, we need to start playing offense with our lives." I LOVE THAT! What is it that you are afraid of? What is it that masters you? When we live for God, He gives us boldness. So what are some things that are mastering you? Is it the fear of people? Do you spend too much time worrying about what people will think about you? Is it the fear of failure? Theodore Roosevelt said, "The only man who never makes a mistake is the man who never does anything." Do not allow fear to rob you of the vision that God has birthed in your soul. Do you fear trying new things? Do you fear losing what you have? I don't know what it is you fear, but if fear is your master then it is a sign that Jesus is not.

Let's Wrap This Bad Boy Up

So what does all of this have to do with the title of this book? Great question. Ultimately, being a certified people pleasure is about fear. It's about fearing what others think about you. It's about fearing what others might say about you. It's about fearing man more than fearing God. One brings anguish; the other brings life.

Knowing whose you are means that you know God. You need to know that God is holy and worthy of our fear. He deserves our respect. Our love for Him should outweigh our fear of pleasing people. We can trust that even if someone mistreats us, or doesn't respond well when we say that God is a good God and bigger than any human. We have to stop being afraid of people's opinions I can't tell you how many times I haven't taken a holy risk because I was afraid of what someone might say. What if I fail? What if people don't understand? What if someone makes fun of me? That's fear! I wonder how times we make fear decisions and not faith decisions. When we make decisions out of fear of man, it causes us to miss out on God. I believe that far too many of us fear what we should fear not, and we don't fear what we should fear.

To live for God means that we have a holy fear of God. It means we can trust that God is good. It means that when it comes to man's approval, we should fear not. Before you move on from this chapter, ask yourself the following questions:

- Do I fear man over God?
- What would it take for me to fear God more than I fear man?
- What Godly risk would I do right now If I knew that I couldn't fail?

Chapter Eighteen

You Can't Force Fruit

As a Christian, I am supposed to produce spiritual fruit. You know things like love, joy, peace etc. The fruit producing can make a book like this frustrating. You know what a Christian is supposed to look like, but for some reason no life change happens. You don't want to be addicted to pleasing people, but even after reading 18 chapters on a book dedicated to this subject, you haven't seen much change. The problem is that many Christians focus on the fruit.

Christians know that they should produce love, so they will within themselves that they are going to love more. That lasts for about a nanosecond because someone that is hyper annoying will enter the room and you will want to punch them in the throat repeatedly until a narrator with a deep voice yells, "Finish him!" You will then want to do things that are straight out of the video game *Mortal Kombat* and that is not very loving.

Christians know that they are supposed to be patient. They feel bad when they are not, so they sing, "We need a little patience...

yeah-ah" by Guns N Roses and then hope for the best. What happens? Traffic. Traffic makes me think and say things aloud that are not very Christian. If other drivers would just submit to me, I would have a lot less frustration while driving. I'm betting you have had a similar thought. Joy. Christians should be filled with an unexplainable joy. For most though, joy is like a roller coaster and it goes up and down.

Christians know that they should put God first and seek to please him, yet we spend most of our time keeping up with the Jones, fighting for our rights, and living to please people. Reading a book will help, but it won't produce fruit. I love the quote by JD Greear:

> **Spiritual fruit is produced in the same way physical fruit is. When a man and woman conceive physical fruit ie a child, they are usually not thinking about the mechanics of making that child. Rather they get caught up in the moment of loving intimacy with one another and the fruit of that loving intimacy is a child.**

Now, for Monica and me, physical fruit was difficult to produce. We went for six years before God blessed us with kids. At one point I had to give Monica shots, she had to take her temperature every day and chart it, and then when her temperature hit a certain point, we had to cue the Boys II Men music.

The only problem was that the doctor ordered us to do it. And when I say do it, I mean a lot in a short amount of time. If you are a guy you might think that this sounds like the best week ever…BUT IT WASN'T! Oh, and there was no Boys II Men music, or if you are a little older, Marvin Gaye. At one point I told Monica that I wasn't a machine. The joy of producing physical fruit became frustrating because we focused on the fruit and not on the love.

Most Christians do the same thing.

They focus on the fruit of love, joy, peace, patience, kindness, goodness, gentleness, and self-control, and when they cannot produce these things they get frustrated. Not only does focusing on the fruit become frustrating, it also becomes a burden. It is such a heavy burden that many people end up faking the fruit. They pretend to be a better Christian than they really are.

The key to producing spiritual fruit is to stop focusing on the fruit and start focusing on Jesus. When we abide in Jesus (It literally means to make our home in Him), He naturally produces in us spiritual fruit. Love produces fruit. Focusing on fruit produces frustration.

"Abide in Me, and I in you. As the branch cannot bear fruit of itself unless it abides in the vine, so neither can you unless you abide in Me." (John 15:4)

Did you catch what Jesus said? He said that you cannot bear fruit unless you abide in Him. That means that you cannot just will your way to living for God. You cannot just clench your fists, grunt, and then, poof, you are changed. I wonder how many of us are trying to produce fruit without abiding in Jesus?

Jesus also says, "I am the vine, you are the branches; he who abides in Me and I in him, he bears much fruit, for apart from Me you can do nothing" (John 15:5).

Jesus says something that often gets misquoted here. He says that apart from me you can do nothing. I've heard that taught as in you literally cannot do anything without Jesus, but that simply is not true. You can do a lot without Jesus and that is the problem. You can work hard and make a lot of money and not even believe in Jesus. You can become disciplined and be up in the gym just working on your fitness. You can get buff without Jesus. You can even grow a church without Jesus. When you put this verse in context with what Jesus is saying, He's not saying that you cannot do anything. He is saying that you can't grow fruit. If you want to feel intimacy with Jesus, it is not going to happen without Him. If you want God to change your life, it is not going to happen without Jesus. You can do a lot of stuff without Jesus, but you can't abide in Jesus without Jesus. You can't experience the life that Jesus promised without abiding in Him.

Sometimes when I'm struggling with something, I have to preach to myself about Jesus. Sometimes I am really hard on myself. I start thinking that I'm not good enough. I start thinking that God won't use me to reach people through Next Level Church because I've messed up. Sometimes I simply have to allow my mind to abide in Jesus. I have to make my mind make a home in Jesus. When I'm being really negative, I often quote to myself a verse from the Bible "Whatever is true, whatever is noble, whatever is right, or pure, if it is lovely, if it is admirable, if it is excellent or praiseworthy think about such things." Sometimes I have spent so much time abiding in worldly thinking that it just messes me up. Sometimes I have to just abide in Jesus by thinking about what He did for me. God's not mad at me. God does not hate me. God loves me. God has a plan for me. God is proud of me. God does not see me as a dirty rotten sinner who keeps messing up. God sees me as His perfect son. Jesus is like Pringles. You can't eat just one. When you spend time thinking about Jesus, talking to God, reading about Him, and singing to Him, it puts a taste in your mouth and spurs you on to grow fruit. Let's keep reading and see how Jesus ends this section.

> If you abide in Me, and My words abide in you, ask whatever you wish, and it will be done for you. My Father is glorified by this, that you bear much fruit, and so prove to be My disciples. Just as the Father has loved Me, I have also loved you; abide in My love. If you keep My commandments, you will abide in My love; just as I have kept My Father's

commandments and abide in His love. These things I have spoken to you so that My joy may be in you, and that your joy may be made full (John 15:7-11).

Jesus says that if you abide in Him, you will bear much fruit. Jesus then says to ask whatever you wish and it will be done for you. Well, maybe Jesus means that if you want to win the lottery pray to Him and He will win it for you, or maybe in context of this verse He will give you something greater than the lottery! Jesus will give you Himself. He will abide in you. There are times when I don't feel like worshiping God, and in those times, I ask God to change my heart. I know that unless my heart is changed, I'll never seek God.

We can bear fruit because Jesus loves us. He tells us to abide in His love. This is where so many of us miss it. We abide in his rules. We start with wanting to be better, so we strap up our laces and declare that this week we are going to be better. Instead, we need to focus on Jesus' love for us. We need to find our home in Him. Jesus ends this section by saying that when we do this, our joy will be made full! I don't know about you, but that's what I want! I want to have true joy. I don't want to fake it. I want to truly enjoy being with Jesus and have His joy radiate through me. Make your home in Him. For some of you, that means that you just need to carve out time for Him. You may really enjoy praying, but you have just been abiding in way too much TV. Some of you just need to download some worship music and listen to it in your car. You need to abide in Jesus on your way to work. Some of you need to spend less time on your Facebook and more time on your face before God. You'll never find your identity in Jesus if you don't abide in Jesus. It's through Jesus that we can learn to please God more than man. I don't know what you need to do to abide in Jesus, but I hope that you will be spurred on to do it. It's only through Jesus that we can truly be set free from pleasing people.

Chapter Nineteen

Now You Can Become
a People Pleaser

Now you are ready to become a people pleaser. Do what?! I know this is going to take a little explaining. The goal of this book is not that we would become anti-people. It's that we would find our identity in Jesus. Once you know who you are in Christ, it frees you from the trap of pleasing people. Like most things in life, people pleasing can be bad and good. It's bad when it controls us and ultimately is all about us. Think about it, when you are obsessed to please people it is often about making yourself look good. You do not want someone to think less of you so you aim to please people. That is selfish and unhealthy. It's healthy when it's done out of a response for what God has done in your life. Don't get confused. Stick with me on this one.

The Apostle Paul without a doubt knew who he was in Jesus. His identity was secure. He made it clear that his first call was to please

God and not man. At the same time, he makes it clear that he will do whatever it takes to win people to Jesus. Look at what Paul says,

> Though I am free and belong to no one, I have made myself a slave to everyone, to win as many as possible. To the Jews I became like a Jew, to win the Jews. To those under the law I became like one under the law (though I myself am not under the law), so as to win those under the law. To those not having the law I became like one not having the law (though I am not free from God's law but am under Christ's law), so as to win those not having the law. To the weak I became weak, to win the weak. I have become all things to all people so that by all possible means I might save some. I do all this for the sake of the gospel that I may share in its blessings (Corinthians 9:19-23).

So Paul makes himself a slave to everyone. At first glance, that may seem contradictory to being free in Jesus. We've spent 18 chapters trying to become free from the slavery of people pleasing, and now all of a sudden we are supposed to please people! Yes…once you find your identity in Jesus, then you live to share God's salvation with everyone. It's kind of like this, when I go to a party, I want to lose my identity in Jesus. I don't want to misrepresent my church, family, or God. Therefore, I'm not going to get plastered drunk and start fist pumping like I'm on an episode of "The Jersey Shore" just so I can fit in. Falling to peer pressure is being a people pleaser. What I am going to do is try to connect with people where they are. Because I'm secure in who I belong to, I do not have to make the party all about me. I can get out of the way and connect with people where they are. I will talk sports with the sports fans. Even though I HATE politics I'll talk politics with the political people. We all know just how fun a political party is. Get it? If

I'm at a party and everyone is talking about their kids, then I'm going to talk about why parents blame everything on their baby's teething. Seriously! Parents blame every temper tantrum, fever, bad night's sleep, and the teenage years on teething. I digress. Now my identity is not found in the people I connect with. I still am me. I still am who God has created me to be. I am simply getting out of the way of myself so that I can connect with people for the sake of Jesus.

Here is something that I have discovered. People love to talk about themselves. I love people because Jesus loves me. Because I love people, I ultimately want all people to know Jesus. One of the best ways I've discovered how to get to know people is to have them talk about themselves. I find something that we have in common and then get out of the way. I try to let them talk. The amazing thing is that most people will eventually turn the table back to you. When they do, it opens the door for me to share my faith.

Please don't read this as me making people a project. I truly care about people. I want to know people and where they are. Paul says that he becomes all things to all people so that he might save some. My goal is not to cram Jesus down someone's throat. It's to get to know people so that they know that I care about them. I want to fiercely love people to Jesus. I will do my best to care about what they care about because they matter to God, and therefore, they matter to me.

Application

Who do you know that needs Jesus? Pray for them. Specifically pray that God will give you an opportunity to tell them about Jesus. Now go and love people where they are. Love them even if they aren't interested in Jesus. Become all things to all people so that you can win some for Jesus. Once you've found your identity in Jesus then you are ready to become a people pleaser.

Chapter Twenty

I'm Still Not Perfect

I'm still not perfect at resisting the urge to please people. Like a drug addict, I'll probably never be cured. I know how to resist it, and I know what I need to do. I've come along way. I've written this book. I've preached lots of sermons. I have memorized lots of verses, but I'm still not perfect at it. I'm just as much in need of God's love, grace, and forgiveness today. The point of this book is not to make us perfect. The point of this book is to open our eyes to how much we desperately need God. We need God if we are ever going to have peace with ourselves and with others. We need God period.

On my good days, I brush off the words from other people. I see past their negativity because I understand that hurt people hurt people. On my good days, I forgive those who have wronged me. However, even on my best days, I'm not perfect. I'm not perfect, especially on my bad days. There have been times where negative thoughts have been so powerful I felt like I was being consumed. In the moment, I don't see it as a spiritual attack. When my mind goes negative, it becomes the Terminator killing every good thought in its wake.

When I was in college, I memorized a verse that does more than help me. When my mind goes negative, I quote this verse. Sometimes, I quote it more than once. Sometimes, I say it out loud, over and over again until I've taken my negative thoughts captive. The Bible is an awesome weapon of mass instruction. It tells us what to do when our brain turns on us.

> Finally brothers, whatever is true, whatever is noble, whatever is right, whatever is pure, whatever is lovely, whatever is admirable—if anything is excellent or praiseworthy—think about such things. Whatever you have learned or received or heard from me, or seen in me—put it into practice. And the God of peace will be with you (Philippians 4:8-9).

Paul ended his amazingly encouraging letter to the Philippians with this challenge. The challenge is to think about whatever is true, noble, right, pure, lovely, admirable, excellent, and praiseworthy. When I'm hit with negativity that is brought on by other imperfect people or brought on by my own brain, I stand on this verse. If it's not true, right, pure, lovely, admirable, excellent, or praiseworthy, I don't want to think about it. In fact, I want what this verse promises—the peace of God.

I figure that if these words are good enough for Paul to use to end his letter, they are more than good enough for me to end this book. Whether it's negative thoughts about yourself or negative thoughts about others, remember that your identity is in Jesus. When you feel attacked, remember, *Even if you were perfect, someone would crucify you.* When others lash out, remember to forgive them because you have been forgiven. Remember that hurt people hurt people. Show hurt people grace and confess to others when you hurt them. If you forget everything that's in this book, please never forget to continually think about whatever is true, noble, right, pure, lovely, admirable, excellent, or praiseworthy. May the only perfect Savior, crucified for your sake, guard your heart and your mind forever.

CPSIA information can be obtained at www.ICGtesting.com
Printed in the USA
BVOW040317120613

323084BV00002B/98/P